Light without Fire

Light without Fire

The Making of America's First Muslim College

Scott Korb

BEACON PRESS
BOSTON

Beacon Press
25 Beacon Street
Boston, Massachusetts 02108-2892
www.beacon.org

Beacon Press books
are published under the auspices of
the Unitarian Universalist Association of Congregations.

16   15   14   13   8   7   6   5   4   3   2   1

This book is printed on acid-free paper that meets the uncoated paper ANSI/NISO
specifications for permanence as revised in 1992.

Text design by Ruth Maassen

Excerpts from the poems "Spring's Gift," by Hamza Yusuf Hanson, "History 101,"
by Zaid Shakir, and "Book," by Rasheeda Plenty, are printed here with the permis-
sion of their authors.

Library of Congress Cataloging-in-Publication Data

Korb, Scott.
  Light without fire : the making of America's first Muslim college / Scott Korb.
    p. cm.
  ISBN 978-0-8070-0163-9 (alk. paper)
  1. Zaytuna College (Berkeley, Calif.)—History. 2. Islamic universities and colleges—
California—Berkeley—History. I. Title.
  BP43.U62Z394 2012
  297.071'179467—dc23
                              2012043449

For Kate and Walker

God is the light of the heavens and the earth. The likeness of His light is of as a niche with a lamp inside; the lamp is in a glass; the glass is as a shining star, like from a blessed olive tree, neither of the East nor of the West, its oil nearly luminous even without fire touching it.

—Koran 24:35

CONTENTS

11/5/09, "Going Muslim"

My views are actually quite mainstream.

—Tunku Varadarajan

Sometimes I can be really *slow*. Like the fact that it took me till around the middle of sophomore year to finally get the escalator business at Stuy straight: All the escalators that go up start from the east side. All the escalators that go down start from the west side.

—Ebadur Rahman

On November 9, 2009, the journalist and magazine editor Tunku Varadarajan published an essay in *Forbes* responding to the mass shooting, four days before, by military psychiatrist Nidal Malik Hasan at the Army base in Fort Hood, Texas. While it would not be exactly fair to call Varadarajan a colleague—we've only ever corresponded, and this only very recently—that fall semester he was teaching at New York University's Stern School of Business, a stone's throw from where I was teaching a writing seminar about religion at NYU's Gallatin School of Individualized Study. Our proximity seemed reason enough to take his essay somewhat personally; so did the fact that we both drew paychecks from the same big account—though it wasn't just that.

Certainly most of us can recall the terrible facts about Fort Hood: Thirty people were injured and thirteen people killed; nearly all of the dead were military personnel. Various reports from the scene had Hasan, a Muslim, calling out *"Allahu akbar!"* before his rampage. *Allahu akbar* means "God is the greatest." In the years that followed, I'd hear this exclamation, known as the *takbir*, more times than I could report.

Varadarajan's headline alone—"Going Muslim"—told the story that he believed alarmingly too few Americans were willing to tell. Playing, of course, on the notion of "going postal," Varadarajan was attempting to coin this phrase as a way to "describe the turn of events where a seemingly integrated Muslim-American . . . discards his apparent integration into American society and elects to vindicate his religion in an act of messianic violence against his fellow Americans." The scenario—enacting quintessential Islam, he appeared to be saying—seemed even more dangerous than threats of "homegrown terror" for being both unpredictable and inevitable. Things that grow—plants, molds, children—develop over time, usually in ways we can see; "going Muslim" could happen in an instant, without fair warning. And what's worse, by Varadarajan's account, the fact that it wasn't happening every day seemed to go against the very nature of the Muslim, whose vindication in the contemporary West could only be earned by murder.

These claims led to some controversy around school—angry students and faculty, calls for disciplinary action against Varadarajan, and defenses of him on the grounds of academic freedom. A response from the dean of the business school, Thomas Cooley, suggested that any offended students simply hadn't thought enough about the piece to understand it. NYU president John Sexton read it and thought enough about it to find it offensive. Jeremy Walton, a professor from the Religious Studies Program, made the case on a university website for considering Varadarajan's essay a piece of hate speech, calling it not just racist but chauvinistic. Walton was not alone.

The controversy was actually a few days old before I heard any word of it or had the chance to read Varadarajan's essay myself. I learned of it from a student, the quiet Muslim Ebadur Rahman, who sat most days at the far corner of the seminar table. He'd asked us to call him Ebad, for short, and having stumbled over both his given and family names while taking attendance the first day of class, I was grateful for that. Up to this point, he'd speak when called on. He'd very occasionally raise his hand with a thought to share. When he did, I would almost always have to ask him to speak up or say again what he'd been saying.

Ebad seemed integrated, though he wore a white skullcap, or *kufi*, and always a plain, loose-fitting button-up shirt. He tried to grow a beard then and still tries today.

Ebad's parents were from Bangladesh. He'd been raised in New York City's East Village and was now living at home. I'd learned by way of a few writing assignments he did for class that growing up he'd struggled with interpretations of Islam—in the mosque, the broader community, even among his family—that seemed to stress the length of a man's beard and the fit of his pants more than anything Ebad would say was particularly "relevant." That was Ebad's favorite word those days. His favorite Muslims were relevant and preached and taught about relevance.

Ebad was older than my other freshmen, which meant that though he was quiet, he didn't exhibit the typical anxieties and insecurities of first-year college students about thinking the right thing, dressing the right way, knowing enough, or saying enough sufficiently smart things in class to impress me. He was eager to please, but not too eager. In time I would come to see his basic soft-spokenness as an expression of humility and deference more than anything else. This was part of his Islam.

In 2004, after graduating from Stuyvesant High School, one of New York's premier public schools, Ebad moved cross-country to enroll in an experimental Islamic seminary program known for a time as the Tabari School of Islamic Studies and run by an organization called Zaytuna Institute. Zaytuna had been founded in 1996 by the American convert Sheikh Hamza Yusuf Hanson and a partner, Hesham al-Alusi, as a nonprofit educational institute. By 1998 they had broken ground on a permanent Bay Area campus off a busy boulevard in Hayward, California. Individuals and whole families arrived by the score. The campus bustled in the evenings all week and during the weekend all day. Hamza oversaw the construction of a yurt and the installation of archery targets high in the trees. Archery was one of the Prophet Muhammad's favorite recreations, and the Muslim tries in all ways to model his life on the life of the Prophet. This also explains Ebad's scant beard and even the concern the community had with the cuffs on trousers.

When the seminary program was established in 2004, nearly a decade after Sheikh Hamza first incorporated the institute, Ebad was one of six students who started in the course—two women, four men—and was one of the five who finished. Sheikh Hamza conceived Zaytuna as an American version of the traditional Islamic madrasah education he'd gotten as a younger man throughout the Middle East and North Africa—particularly among the Bedouins of Mauritania.

Living and studying with the scholars and the rest of a growing community at Zaytuna seemed to have made it clear to Ebad just how much they all knew, especially his teachers, and just how much he had to learn. I'd never known a student to carry more books around with him; each one seemed just one more piece of a puzzle that, *insha'Allah*—"if God wills"—Ebad would say, might continue to reveal what a relevant Islam could look like in America.

His assignments for me often looked, at first, more like pages torn from *Bartlett's Familiar Quotations* than anything he might have properly called his own: "You'll notice and I realize," he once wrote me, "that I still have a number of long quotes that I need to work in better." Why try to say yourself what those before you have said with more knowledge, eloquence, and grace than you can muster? More even than Judaism, Islam places a premium on memorization and the verifiable transmission of wisdom across the generations. It started with Muhammad. Ebad was just doing his part.

For my class Ebad both wrote about and quoted at length the most relevant Muslims he knew, some of whom he had lived and studied with on the Zaytuna campus in California. He told me how Sheikh Hamza, with the help of two other Muslim scholars, was just then transforming the seminary program into a liberal arts college.

It turned out that Ebad's seminary program, which had some trappings of typical Western education, was mainly the brainchild of Imam Zaid Shakir, a black convert originally from Berkeley, who, like Hamza, had studied overseas and returned with ambitions to make Islam indigenous to the United States. And yet, though the seminary was supposedly "at the forefront of Zaytuna's goals" as late as the spring of 2007, the founders and others close to Sheikh Hamza, with

Shakir leading the way, were already planning what would result in a move away from Hayward's Zaytuna Institute and toward a permanent four-year college that they eventually hoped would earn accreditation by the Western Association of Schools and Colleges (WASC). This had all become possible with the arrival in 2003 of Imam Zaid, who, by Ebad's telling, came across as the most relevant of all.

Not only did Imam Zaid preach and write about American Islam—"This is indeed our country," Ebad had more than once transcribed—other Muslims were already writing about him in historic terms. In a poem called "Can I Marry Your Daughter?" the spoken-word artist Dasham Brookins, aka Brother Dash, makes a comparison that Ebad and many other Zaytunies—their preferred term of endearment—have made over the years: "I'll teach her about a people that gave birth to Malcolm *and* Imam Zaid." The comparison to Malcolm X, known at the end of his life as El-Hajj Malik El-Shabazz, is not one you'll hear from Zaid himself—"because," as religion journalist Laurie Goodstein reported in 2006 for the *New York Times*, "he so often preaches the importance of humility." For her report about the seminary program, Goodstein interviewed Ebad, "a son of Bangladeshi immigrants in New York City who chose Zaytuna over the Ivy League": "Sheikh Hamza and Imam Zaid have grown up here after having studied abroad, and you can really connect with them," said the New Yorker, Ebadur Rahman, who is nineteen. "The scholars who come from abroad, they can't connect with the people. They're ignorant of life here."

After four years in Hayward, Ebad returned to New York. And here, at home, a few days after another Muslim, this one a member of the US Army, had once again killed a number of Americans, a professor at his university seemed to be suggesting that his classmates and his teachers, including me, remain vigilant against the likes of him. Be wary. Why? Because. "Their religion," Varadarajan claimed, "is founded on bellicose conquest, a contempt for infidels and an obligation for piety that is more extensive than in other schemes."

In the few months I'd known him, Ebad had sure never seemed bellicose or full of contempt. His extensive piety—revealed occasionally, say, in some reference to daily prayers or of having studied at a semi-nary, something I'd also done—always seemed balanced with good humor and a kind of skepticism, especially where other people's piety ran afoul of relevance. And unlike the pious believers I've known from those religious traditions Varadarajan refers to as "other schemes," Ebad wasn't the least bit judgmental. Perhaps piously so. After all, ac-cording to a translation by Sheik Hamza himself, tradition has it that the Prophet Jesus said: "Leave humanity alone, and by doing so, give them repose from yourself. Always occupy yourself with good against the evil of yourself. Leave humanity, neither seeking their praise nor earning their censure. Concern yourself with what has been entrusted to you." In other words, Jesus says mind your own business; the Mus-lims are supposed to listen.

As a class we'd talked only briefly about the Fort Hood killings the week after the shooting had happened. In those days just after midterm I'd scheduled readings about Reinhold Niebuhr, the mid-century theologian most celebrated in his own day for pointing out that the irony of American history rested in recognizing our real culpability in becoming a world power, in seeing that we were far less innocent than our theories of democracy, free market capital-ism, militarism, and evangelicalism assumed. Despite a brief interest in Niebuhr among certain political writers around the 2008 elec-tions, today he's probably still most well known for having written the Serenity Prayer. Since 9/11 especially, though, Niebuhr's ideas of American culpability in the world have been caricatured as the philo-sophical underpinning of a "blame America first crowd." Suffice it to say, I wasn't at the moment tuned in enough to see how the massacre at Fort Hood might have dovetailed with my lesson for the week. And so, after a few minutes—the body count, the fact that Hasan was a Muslim, that details were still coming in—we moved on. Ebad had remained typically quiet during that discussion.

But before class the next week, Ebad brought Varadarajan's ar-ticle to my attention and forced the issue, albeit politely—my own schedule and lesson plan be damned.

In class, we read the piece aloud, each student taking a paragraph before passing off the responsibility to the next one. Even I took a turn. It was strange having Varadarajan's words in my mouth. I'm not usually quite this paranoid:

> The difference between "going postal," in the conventional sense, and "going Muslim," in the sense that I suggest, is that there would not necessarily be a psychological "snapping" point in the case of the imminently violent Muslim; instead, there could be a calculated discarding of camouflage—the camouflage of integration—in an act of revelatory catharsis.

Though his rhetoric seemed more far-reaching than this—it seemed to reach into my classroom—in the end, the only practical bit of advice Varadarajan proposed was to the armed forces and involved mandatory reporting of suspicious remarks or behavior up the chain of command, and the addition of some Pentagon-level officials to review these reports so they could act on them in real time. Fortunately, the essay wasn't long enough to have Ebad take a turn. He just sat and took it while his classmates told him how dangerous he was—a point of fact that since 9/11 was hardly news to him.

Very soon after the attacks of September 2001, Annie Thoms, an English teacher at New York's Stuyvesant High School, began talking with the Stuyvesant Theater Community about their annual production known as the Winter Drama. She had a plan. Cut off from her students in the days after the attacks—they'd be out of classes until September 20, when they began meeting at a rival high school in Brooklyn, not to return to Stuyvesant until October 9—she'd been perusing student-run message boards, where she found scores of posts detailing Stuyvesant students' various responses to what they witnessed that day from their school, which was located just four blocks away from Ground Zero. "This meant," Thoms has written, "hundreds of Stuyvesant students saw the planes hit, saw people jumping from office windows, saw the towers fall." Thoms had ascended from the subway as she did every day, and the whole world was looking up. She joined them.

The reactions Thoms found online in those early days, before finally rejoining her students for several weeks of classes at Brooklyn

Technical High School, began to coalesce for her into an idea for "a play in which Stuyvesant students were able to tell their own stories, and the stories of others." The cast was chosen and interviews began November 12, 2001, the same day the world stopped again as an American Airlines flight fell from the sky into a neighborhood in the Rockaways section of Queens. (On that morning, I happened to be traveling from Milwaukee to Newark, New Jersey; after the plane made a drastic turn midflight, several of my fellow passengers unlocked seatback phones and swiped credit cards and repeated in hushed tones to their loved ones: "An explosion?" "New York?" "Another crash?")

Thoms's play came together over the next few months. Each cast member interviewed two or three people and created a script based on their stories, in the model of playwright and actor Anna Deavere Smith's groundbreaking *Fires in the Mirror*, a play about the 1991 riots in Crown Heights, Brooklyn, that erupted after a black boy was killed on his bike and a Jewish student was stabbed.

Ebad was a sophomore at Stuyvesant on 9/11, and not long ago he gave me his copy of the play. *With Their Eyes* was published in 2002, with a foreword by Smith. Ebad's copy of the book is, unsurprisingly, annotated with the fine pencil lines I know from handwritten work he did for my class. What's surprising, though, is what he's chosen to annotate—hardly at all the narratives of the students or a safety agent, an English teacher, or a building contractor. No, Ebad has scribbled, occasionally in Arabic, throughout the chronology and the original production notes from the play. From 9:51 to 10:29 a.m., the chronology reads, "Students are joined on their walk uptown by pedestrians fleeing lower Manhattan, many covered head-to-toe with dust." About those covered in ash, Ebad has scratched: "I didn't notice / don't remember." On the book's entry for September 20, when Stuyvesant reopened at Brooklyn Tech with an assembly in the huge auditorium, Ebad recalls in the margins, "Outside FBI." The production notes explain that *With Their Eyes* "was performed at Stuyvesant High School on February 8 and 9, 2002." Sometime in the years that followed, Ebad wondered, "Where was I, / disconnected from, did I know, hear about? care?"

The morning of 9/11, a fourteen-year-old Ebad was in Eric Grossman's second-period European literature class when principal Stanley Teitel came over the public-address system with preliminary word of the attacks and instructions for the students of Stuyvesant. At the end of Grossman's class, Ebad moved through the library on the sixth floor and looked down through the windows; he'd never seen the Greenway along the Hudson River so filled with people. Moving up the West Side stairwell toward his drafting classroom on the tenth floor, before eventually being directed to gather with other students in his homeroom on the ninth, Ebad had the same view again, those same people fleeing north from the burning buildings to the south.

It was only minutes before Stuyvesant would begin to spill out onto the streets, as well. Two girls Ebad knew from his homeroom, Tarnima and Liana, held hands as they moved along the Hudson River Greenway. He was asked by another friend, Umer, whether he was okay. *Was anyone?* Together they all walked for a while.

Ebad's apartment in the East Village wasn't so far from the school, though, and at a point he decided to peel off and find his way there alone. It didn't occur to him that Umer, or any of his other friends, might like to accompany him, might like a place to get away from all this.

As he was in the habit of doing those days, while walking home across the city Ebad listened to a recording of a recitation of the Koran by Sheikh Ali Huzaifi, imam of the Prophet's Mosque in Medina. He was in the middle of memorizing the twelfth chapter of the Koran on 9/11; by December or January Ebad would have the whole scripture memorized, an accomplishment that earns a Muslim the designation of *haafiz.*

"I remember thinking," he's since reflected, "that people might see it strange that I was listening to my Walkman music while everything and everyone was in chaos."

Of course, it might have been worse had those people known he was listening to the Koran: "The evil-doers could not be saved from Our scourge. Their annals point a moral to men of understanding. This is no invented tale, but a confirmation of previous scriptures, an explanation of all things, a guide and a blessing to true believers." Believers like Ebad.

Ebad has never fully described for me his experience of being so close to so much destruction and death that day. "I don't think I was mature enough to understand 9/11 when it happened," he's reflected. He's even wondered what it might have been like had he not left Umer and the two girls behind. "I definitely missed out on experiences other people had that day." One experience he missed was reported in a special 9/11 issue of the *Spectator*, Stuyvesant's school paper: "According to senior Naazia Husain, a pedestrian who passed her group of diverse Stuyvesant students dining at 23rd Street said, 'Look at the Palestinians celebrating.'" Ebad told me about a history teacher at the school, Anthony Valentin, who wrote of a similar experience inside the school itself, after he met two Muslim girls in the hallways as the place was emptying out. Valentin described this encounter in a piece he called "Diary of a Stuyvesant Teacher: A Muslim Point of View":

> As I walked up the stairs, I came across two female students who were crying. One of these students was wearing traditional Muslim attire. I asked if they were okay and the most-composed student said "yes," but told me that students were making accusatory comments insinuating that the WTC disaster was a terrorist attack by Muslims. I told the student that was crying that I too was a Muslim and that Allah will be with us all. I attempted to remind her that the Lord would not abandon her or any one of us. He knows all and knows best.

Soon after arriving home, Ebad left again for his local mosque. He took his bike, a simple choice he would later recall while writing a farewell message to members of the Stuyvesant Muslim Student Association in the days before his 2004 high school graduation. "Until recently (because the chain, gears, and everything is messed up)," he typed out, "I've mostly gone to the masjid on bike. When it was time for the noon prayer on that day, I got on my bike and went." Unlike with his thinking about the recitation playing over his Walkman, Ebad didn't seem especially aware in the moment of how his ride to the mosque might have appeared to other New Yorkers still reeling in the hours after the Towers fell. Writing in 2004 to his friends in the MSA, Ebad had a different perspective: "People must have seen that as not nice at all, me having a Happy Bike Day 2001 when this had happened."

This new self-consciousness and Ebad's increased awareness of the Muslim's suspect place in American life would develop in unison after 9/11. By the time of his American literature course in the fall of 2002, Ebad had begun to feel the eyes of the world on him. He fell in love with the Transcendentalists, especially Emerson's essay "Self-Reliance": "For non-conformity the world whips you with its displeasure," Emerson had written. Ebad streaked this line with a yellow highlighter and noted: "I can relate to . . . being looked at as diff. from everyone else—especially nowadays."

Emerson: "The by-standers look askance on him in the public street or in the friend's parlour."
Ebad: "On the train . . ."

Thoughts like these—awareness of being always on the defensive, feeling as though his very existence as a Muslim was displeasing to the world around him—were in large part what prompted Ebad to enroll in Zaytuna's pilot seminary program when he graduated from Stuyvesant. He was looking for ways both to ground himself more deeply in Islam and, though he may not have put it this way then, to present himself culturally as a faithful American Muslim. His success in this at the seminary would end up sending me to Zaytuna, too. I needed to see where Ebad had come from.

It may be that attacks carried out by so-called integrated Muslims in the years since 9/11 have made Tunku Varadarajan feel his warning was proper, and properly put. What do you say in the face of under-wear bombers flying over Detroit or, in the months just before Zaytuna opened, a smoking Nissan Pathfinder abandoned in Times Square and loaded with fireworks and propane tanks, gasoline, and 250 pounds of fertilizer? Here, in essence, is the problem I faced the day we looked at Varadarajan's essay in my religion class—a problem that gets to the very heart of what you're about to read. Like many writers I know, I teach writing. And I tend, as much as possible, to teach what I know. It's no coincidence that this tendency in teaching mirrors the writer's maxim: "Write what you know." In the past I've done this.

My own background and religious training was in Christian theology, which over the years I'd paired with a fair sampling of Judaism. I've studied Torah with a rabbi and wrote my first book with a moderately religious Jew, who taught me a great deal about the oldest of the three great monotheisms. While a student at Union Theological Seminary in the years before 9/11, I'd taken a required course on Islam but was preoccupied most of that term writing a novel I never published. One assignment I remember had me respond to the ranting of a lunatic Muslim I'd never heard of before: Osama bin Laden.

With the present book, which begins with a story of a Muslim in my own college classroom and, as you'll see, is essentially about what happens with Muslims in other college classrooms, I set out to write something I didn't know. It sounds absurd, but as late as 2009 I was attempting to teach students how to think deeply and write well about contemporary American religion without really being knowledgeable enough to do it myself.

At the very least, I decided, I could read Varadarajan's words aloud. Over the week that followed I could agree in my gut with every criticism leveled against him. But when Ebad looked to me—and all eyes in the class seemed to follow his in this instance—to do my job as a professor of religion, I could do little more than stare blankly back. In effect, I was handing the class over to him.

I can't help you, I seemed to be saying. *Explain yourself.*

Finding ways to explain himself is what sent Ebadur Rahman to Zaytuna Institute in the first place. Explaining themselves as traditional Muslim scholars is also what Sheikh Hamza Yusuf, Imam Zaid Shakir, and a third founder, Dr. Hatem Bazian, have in mind with Zaytuna College, which, after years of planning, finally opened its doors for the fall semester 2010. Because as much as many of those involved in the story that follows would like to deny it, or like it not to be the case, there's no getting around the central place that the 9/11 terrorist attacks have in the way we—all of us, Muslim and non-Muslim alike—think about the place of Islam in contemporary America. We'd seen it once again at Fort Hood. What we'd been hearing in news report after news report for nearly a decade is that where Muslims gather—in the public square, a local mosque, or a military base loaded with guns—Allah is in their midst, raising Cain.

When Zaytuna College opened its doors, I was there. And I was there again and again throughout that first year—in the classroom, with Rasheeda and Faatimah and Leenah, Mahassin and Sumaya, most, but not all, of these women wearing hijabs. I was in the mosque with Dustin listening to the sermons of Imam Zaid; in Islamic centers tucked away in low-rent industrial parks with Omar and his kids; and in the dormitories and Zaytuna library with Haroon and Chris and Ahmad and Hadeel. We ate together at halal restaurants and celebrated the birth of the Prophet almost every visit. Where Muslims gather, Allah is in their midst. This much I now know is true.

ONE

Zaytunah

Olives (*zaytunah*) are second only to figs in Berg's table of
purifying foods.

—Zaytuna College, "What's in Our Name?"

Without enlightened educational institutions that attract
talented students and in the absence of curricula that impart
a mature understanding of modern thought and realities, it
is unlikely that a sophisticated understanding of the Islamic
religious tradition can ever be fostered.

—Dr. Umar Faruq Abd-Allah

This Sunday afternoon, August 8, 2010, Imam Zaid Shakir was
plugged in, white Apple earbuds matching his white kufi, which, as I
saw it, announced a certain relevance with nothing more than how he
waited around campus drinking coffee. Zaid is remarkably lean and
tall, even seated there at the picnic-style table outside Caffe Strada,
where the summer school students took their breaks from class. He
wore a light-blue striped shirt, buttoned high under his Adam's apple. He was with Muslim friends.

Soon I'd be joining the imam and the summer Zaytunies on a hike
into the Strawberry Canyon of the Berkeley Hills up behind Memo-
rial Stadium, where the views across the bay and into San Francisco
were meant to remind us all of the majesty and unmistakable reality of
Allah. Ebad, who'd invited me to join on the hike, had been in Berkeley most of the summer teaching in an intensive Arabic program, the
first courses offered by Zaytuna in its incarnation as an accreditation-
seeking American college. It had been months since I'd seen Ebad
in New York, and now he was heading back there that very evening,
back to his parents, back to his own college, where we'd met. In the

meantime Ebad would make whatever introductions I'd need into the little *ummah*, the community of the Muslims—including Imam Zaid.

While Zaid was finishing his coffee, some sixty students had gathered, many of them among the imam's most devoted fans, collectors of his recorded sermons and hangers on his every word. They had been living and taking classes together at the Westminster House dormitories at the base of the Hills and across Bancroft Way from the University of California at Berkeley's Law School. When I met him at the doors to Westminster, Ebad introduced me around a little—to Mohammad, a college student from Dayton, Ohio; to Thomas, whose Chicago-based investment firm had sent him here to learn Arabic so he could deal with clients in the Middle East; and finally to Imam Zaid and another Arabic teacher, Imam Dawood Yasin. In the past few years, hikes like this were typically led by Imam Dawood, a onetime fashion model formerly known as David Howard, who'd come to Islam in 1996 after a near-death experience while working in South Africa. Dawood Yasin, a black convert whose Arabic surname comes from a *surah*, or chapter, known to Muslims as the heart of the Koran, had taken over as the imam of a congregation Zaid left behind in New Haven when he came to Zaytuna Institute in Hayward as a scholar-in-residence in 2003. These days, he spent the summers in the Bay Area with his mentor. Dawood, who would one day tell me that a recording of the surah Yasin had brought him to tears even before he could understand Arabic, is younger and sturdier than Zaid. Parts of the hike would be steep.

The group would stretch before starting the climb. Grab your ankle and pull. Then switch. A woman named Thoba (which sounds like "tuba") worried about stretching, unsure she was up for it.

Making a wide circle in a clearing, the students and the two imams joined themselves with arms over each other's shoulders, all the way around. Men made up one half of the circle; women made up the other. Where they would have come together—the men and the women—the circle broke on both sides. At Zaytuna, women and men did not touch.

And yet together, and apart, they swayed. Ebad held tight near his teachers. A new Zaytuna College student, Dustin Craun, a white convert from Denver sporting a goatee who'd been in Berkeley most of the summer rooming with Ebad and studying Arabic in preparation for the start of the school year, tucked himself up against Imam Zaid.

"Brothers and sisters who sway together stay together," said Zaid. That they also prayed together was so obvious it seemed not worth mentioning.

And then up we all went, with Zaid and Dawood in the lead. Dustin took his place in the middle of the pack and kept me company. He'd come to Islam, and Zaytuna specifically, in large part because of his politics, which he said ran "down and to the left," in sharp contrast with a graph he asked me to imagine running endlessly "up and to the right." This was the chart of global capital, the markets, and, to his mind, corruption. Like many academics I know, Dustin sided with those down and out and left behind. Allah was also with the poor.

We talked more about his plans to complete a PhD at UC Berkeley while also working toward a bachelor's degree with Imam Zaid at Zaytuna. Before long, though, we were joined by a bright and beautiful young woman named Ala' Khan, a Berkeley student who'd been spending time with the Zaytunies over the summer. She wore a stud in her nose. Dustin was suddenly preoccupied and would be for much of the rest of the day—indeed, much of the rest of the year.

Just ahead of us was a British student, Zajif Iqbal, telling a few friends, including the investment broker Thomas, about a sermon that he said originated in Yemen and concerned the origins of the first and second thoughts we have when facing a beggar. "The first thought, to give," he said, "comes from God. The second thought, about how much, comes from Shaytan." Shaytan is the devil, and the ease and familiarity with which Zajif spoke about him in that moment gave me the impression that I'd be hearing a lot about Shaytan in the coming days and months. The devil, "the slinking prompter who whispers in the hearts of men," says the Koran, plays an active role in the world of these believers.

Soon after Dustin went off with Ala', I struck up a conversation with a South African woman named Sumaya Jeeva, who, like Zajif and Thoba, was a summer Arabic student and would not be joining the incoming class of the college. Her Arabic was actually quite advanced, and as we proceeded up the hill, I asked and she obliged with a short course on the words and phrases I'd been hearing tossed around even by those Muslims whose general Arabic left something to be desired. I'd heard and read some of this Arabic before, typically in a news report that linked an outburst in Arabic with an outburst of violence. Here's a little of what I learned on the hike. Sumaya used all the words in sentences and offered me an entirely new perspective. (She also followed up with an email.)

Alhamdulillah means "All praise is due to God," as in, "It is a stunning day today, *Alhamdulillah*." Although, it's just as often used in response to the question "How are you?"

Maashaa Allah means "God has willed," and is used especially when praising the appearance of something or someone, as in, "She's a beautiful girl, *maashaa Allah*." It's used this way, Sumaya told me, because all beauty comes from God; beauty is not ours, and saying the phrase helps prevent vanity.

Subhanallah means "Glory be to God," and is often used as an exclamation of awe or admiration, as in, "I had no idea, *subhanallah*, that blah blah blah . . ." or "*Subhanallah*, life is funny; God works in mysterious ways!" Sumaya also told me that a point is made throughout the Koran that everything in heaven and nature is always repeating "subhanallah," which means that everything in creation exists in a constant state of glorifying God. Literally, the word means simply that God is above and beyond all creation.

Allahu akbar means "God is the greatest," and, as Sumaya said, appears regularly in ritual prayers. This was the same *takbir* used at Fort Hood, I recalled. But Sumaya would make me see it in an entirely positive and hopeful light, as a phrase used in moments of amazement or astonishment. At fund-raisers over the course of the year, it would be used when someone promised to give Zaytuna what struck me as a lot of money.

Astaghfirullah means "I seek forgiveness from God." Sumaya suggested that this phrase might be used by a man walking down the street who happened to glance, even inadvertently, at a woman on a magazine cover or billboard. It's also used by someone who has said something he regrets, as in, "No, I shouldn't have said that about her, *astaghfirullah*."

And finally, there's *insha'Allah*, which means "If God wills." This is said whenever someone is referring to anything that might be happening in the future, since in reality, Sumaya said, "We have no idea if we will go to school tomorrow, meet our friends, see our family, marry, have children, finish a degree, and so on. We could die in any second." The injunction comes from the Koran: "Do not say of anything: 'I will do it tomorrow,' without adding: 'If God wills.' When you forget, remember your Lord and say: 'May God guide me and bring me nearer to the Truth.'"

In online social networks, *insha'Allah* is abbreviated "iA."

Following her lesson, Sumaya complained about being basically dissatisfied with the summer Arabic course, in particular with the textbook they used; she would have preferred to have studied Classical Arabic, considered sacred by Muslims. The book they were issued covered Modern Standard Arabic, and was the same version of the language Zaytuna College would be teaching.

Exactly what Arabic the students at Zaytuna would be expected to learn had from the beginning been a central concern of the school. After all, the question of which Arabic to teach raised additional questions: Why are they learning Arabic? Was it for sacred reasons? To help students draw closer to Allah? Or was Zaytuna, as an American liberal arts college, interested in Arabic for modern and practical reasons? To draw its students deeper into the world? What I'd hear from the founders and also in conversation with Ebad and, later, Imam Dawood, and what I'd read in the first-year catalog, suggested that the answer was somewhere in between: "Arabic has become one of the most popular languages taught at American universities, due to the contemporary political importance of the Arab world and because of a growing desire in the West to understand Islam from its original sources. Zaytuna College intends to meet this demand by becoming a preeminent institution for the teaching and study of Arabic."

Despite Islam's long history as a practical, political religion—the Prophet was a political and military leader, after all—Sumaya was not alone in hinting that with this goal in mind, to tackle worldly politics and sacred meaning in one course of study, Zaytuna may have been trying to have the best of both worlds. On its face, this would seem particularly difficult in America, where, as these scholars would agree, Islam itself has no political claim on—and certainly not *over*—the nation's democracy. And yet, as those same scholars would learn in the months to come, the fundamental problem at Zaytuna would not be a curricular one about Arabic's sacred meaning versus its worldly usefulness. Rather, helping these students attain competence in any Arabic at all would become priority number one.

By the time I reached the end of the trail, which led into a hollow at the top of the Hills, Zaid and Dawood had arranged most of the students into another wide circle, all sitting around in the grasses. Zaid had started into a sermon, the first of his I would hear. They were all anticipating the start of the holy month of Ramadan and the fasting it would require.

"During Ramadan we give up good and lawful things, like good, cool water," Zaid said, lifting a plastic bottle from the grass. He likewise gestured to packages of good yogurt balls and lawful Mango Munch in front of him and tossed back a few of these snacks.

"We delight after fasting," he continued, "counting down those last thirty seconds in anticipation: then sip the water and it permeates the body—it diffuses."

Over the past hour I'd overheard conversations anticipating the moon sighting on Wednesday that would start the fast. The weather at midweek might make it difficult for them to see the moon in Berkeley, even from the top of these hills, but beginning with the sighting then or maybe as early as Tuesday, from sunup to sundown during these long days of August and into the first week of September, the Muslims would not eat or drink. And that delight we anticipate during Ramadan, Zaid said, is only the first one. When you eat a date, for example, after a day of fasting, he said, your "mouth almost falls off—like a Kool-Aid smile." (This was a comparison I'd see he was fond of over these weeks.) But the second and greater delight, he said, follows the longing the Muslims have for Allah.

"Like with fasting, you long for it. You long and God longs to meet you." The sermon was becoming a kind of pep talk. Ramadan was not going to be easy. *You can do it.*

Fasting makes us more human in ways we might not expect, he said, by asking us to suppress our physical requirements and the undue attention we often pay to our physical reality. It's that reality, he preached while sitting cross-legged in the grass, that most obviously reveals our differences—a point of fact that led Zaid into a subject dear to his heart: Shaytan, made not of clay but of fire, he said. In the Koran, the devil is said to have claimed a certain distinction between himself and Adam, the first man, based on these physical attributes, which, by Zaid's assessment, made Shaytan "the first racist."

A lesson on the daily longing that comes with a month of fasting had quickly and without warning become a homily about the evils of racism. If fasting as a community makes us more human by reinforcing, in our physical weakness, the robust spiritual and intellectual reality we share, those things that highlight our physical differences do nothing but dehumanize us. Imam Zaid had written about this moment from the Koran, as well: "[Shaytan] says, when ordered to prostrate himself to Adam, *I am better than him. You created me from fire, while you created him from clay*. . . . In addition to his arrogance, his racism is clearly displayed. For the clay that Adam was created from was black in color. . . . Any racist, regardless of his religion, should know he is following in the footsteps of Shaytan in his vile attitudes and practices."

The long hike had left us depleted. All around were young people focused on the physical requirements of water and food and rest. And yet, here was Zaid, asking them not to be so focused. "Ramadan strengthens the heart. And our hearts are strengthened to support the rest of our beings—the intellectual, spiritual," and finally, "the physical." Actually leaning on each other, swaying as they did arm-in-arm before beginning on this hike, does not strengthen the Muslim as much as when the heart is made strong. Tired as everyone seemed—and I certainly felt it in my feet, my legs, my back—Zaid told them they were all stronger and more able to support one another now than when they began. "Like bricks in a wall," he said.

I couldn't help but think that this lesson was somehow relevant to what I'd seen at the bottom of the hill, where the women linked arms and the men linked arms, but the sexes kept themselves from touching while limbering up for the climb. They were together on the hike, but there was this line no one would cross. Zaid seemed to be saying that what separated them physically wasn't nearly as significant as what they shared spiritually and intellectually.

The same would be true of what happened around Zaytuna College; they would pray and study and eat together (no matter what certain pieces of promotional material seemed to say about the college, with its candid images of women sitting at one table and men at another). But the women entering as part of the inaugural class at Zaytuna would not be touched by the men, and vice versa. And the women, as far as Zaid was concerned, would ultimately not become leaders in Islam in the same ways the men might. "We must also understand," he had written in an essay concerning the issue of female prayer leadership, "that Islam has never advocated a strict liberationist philosophy. Our fulfillment in this life will never come as the result of breaking real or perceived chains of oppression. . . . Our fulfillment does not lie in our liberation, rather it lies in the conquest of our own soul and its base desires. . . . When we live for our Lord it becomes easy to live with each other."

Zaid would offer some final thoughts up there in that grove— "Don't curse anyone, because in cursing him you might be cursing a Muslim, and so cursing yourself, even that guy with the wine bottle in the gutter." Muslims aren't supposed to drink. He then recited a poem he'd written called "History 101," which begins with Columbus sailing "the ocean blue" in 1492, then draws connections to the destruction of Hiroshima and Nagasaki, and ends sharply with the state of Islam in America and an ongoing history of genocide in the world:

> Muslims are on the endangered species list.
> Plastic American culture no one can resist.
>
> The holocaust memorial opens to cries of "never again,"
> While Bosnia is being ethnically cleansed.
>
> On and on this story goes,
> So now I'll bring it to a close.

Were you to ask, I'll say, "It's been quite fun!"
Playing ball with history
One-on-one.

Following that, an older Arabic student named Rasheeda Plenty, known in the group as a poet herself, was too shy to share a poem of her own. Though Zaid encouraged her directly, she still declined. Later that afternoon over dinner with a group of students at a House of Curries on Durant Avenue, she would tell me it was still up in the air whether she'd be joining the incoming class of the college. Rasheeda had been with the summer Arabic program for several years now, but having already earned her bachelor's and master's degrees, she wasn't entirely sure whether to start college again at Zaytuna.

Asked to give a few of his own departing thoughts, Ebad, who would be leaving that evening, said only this: "Appreciate the blessings Allah gives us—the Koran, the Arabic language, brothers and sisters."

Then before we all began our descent back to the Westminster House, Zaid took the students through a deep-breathing exercise that he synchronized to the rhythm of the breeze of the Berkeley Hills, to the sounds of nature. As you breathe out, he said, "You say, 'Allah.'" Here it was, *subhanallah*, creation's endless glorification of God.

And then, on the way down, I looked on from behind as Ebad lost his footing on some loose rocks and took a terrible fall; he had to catch himself, since he was surrounded by women who seemed either unable or unwilling—I couldn't be sure—to extend the hand that would have stopped him. He wrapped his arm in a shirt and bled through. He would go home in worse shape than he'd arrived.

In his battered state, Ebad introduced me to a woman named Maryam Kashani, who carried a camera on the hike and explained that only some of the time did she find it necessary to wear a head covering. Most of the other women did most of the time, she said. Originally from San Francisco, Maryam, a Muslim with an Iranian father and a Japanese mother, had been in Berkeley over the summer completing work toward a PhD in anthropology at the University of Texas; her subject was Zaytuna.

Maryam's previous work had been the independent documentary film *Best in the West*, which was released in 2006 and tells the story of her father and a group of his Iranian friends who all moved to San Francisco during the '60s and '70s. Interviewed about the film in 2007 for a website concerned with arts in the Iranian diaspora, she made the point that her film was "a rare opportunity for a young woman to document the lives of an older group of men." When I asked her what one thing I had to be sure to pay close attention to at Zaytuna, she said, "The women."

In that first meeting—and we would have countless others—Maryam also suggested that before long I meet Usama Canon, who'd been around Zaytuna for many years. His Ta'leef Collective, an Islamic community center founded in 2005 as an offshoot of Zaytuna Institute, was especially welcoming to converts.

Ebad led the way back to the Westminster House, where he ducked away for a time to nurse the scrapes he'd suffered on his fall. About ten of us gathered in the hall of the dormitory. Imam Zaid was on his way, too, in need, after the hike, of a place to shower and dress before heading to Santa Clara to raise funds for the Tayba Foundation, an organization developing a distance-learning program for Muslim inmates around the country. This program was named for El-Hajj Malik El-Shabazz, better known as Malcolm X.

The Ohio-native Mohammad, whom I'd met earlier, had offered Imam Zaid the use of his shower and was away scrubbing, it turned out, when Zaid arrived. Then, just as soon as Mohammad emerged from his room, claiming that he would have used rubber gloves had he had just a little more time, the imam disappeared behind the door, comparing himself to Superman in need of a phone booth. He wasn't long.

They all wished they had Imam Zaid around more during the week. It would make him keep his bathroom clean, for one thing, Mohammad said. (And without offering any details, I can confirm that his toilet was disgusting.) That sort of longing for the scholars, a strange covetousness that you don't find at other liberal arts schools, began at the top with Sheikh Hamza, whom I hadn't yet seen but whose name I'd heard mentioned a lot.

The scholars, especially Zaid Shakir and Dawood Yasin during the summer, were part fathers, part teachers, part friends, part super-heroes. And despite the seriousness of their purpose as students and the historic pressure some of them would face as part of the first class of the nation's first Muslim college—so they would attest; so says the Zaytuna literature—the Zaytunies' living situation and some of their shared ideas about the men who led them reflected a certain childish-ness, reminding me at a certain point that some of them really are still kids. Even Dustin, the oldest and most educated student among them, was spending a good deal of his time flirting with Ala', the girl with the nose ring. No crime there, of course.

But then again, things could also get perfectly serious in a moment. Imam Zaid soon returned to join us in the hallway outside Moham-mad's room, refreshed, now wearing a dark suit. Wanting to wish Ebad farewell but finding he was still cleaning up in his room, Imam Zaid said: "He's a good man, Ebad." And after a moment, he continued with thoughts for the rest of us assembled: Dustin and Ala', Thomas and Mohammad, me and a few others still milling about, talking about din-ner. "Islam will enhance our goodness," said Zaid, "if you understand it. If you don't understand it, it can decrease your goodness."

It was as though he couldn't help himself. That word "goodness" required some clarification, a way to make even a passing thought into something more meaningful, in this case an oblique commentary on the destructive, even terrifying, ways Islam is used by extremists and radicals, whose great misunderstanding decreases their goodness immeasurably—concerns, it seems, that like racism and poverty are never far from Imam Zaid's mind. It crossed my mind that Imam Zaid had spent his time in the shower preparing a mini-sermon on the double-edged sword of knowledge.

"A good man," Mohammad agreed. "He had good teachers."

When Ebad finally came from his corner room, clean and prop-erly bandaged, several of us from the hike followed Imam Zaid out to the sidewalk, where he was meeting his wife, who would drive them to the fund-raiser in Santa Clara; he was just now getting off the phone with her. By the time she arrived and they sped off, more than a dozen of us had gathered outside Westminster House, the students making decisions about dinner. For most of them, it was that or the endless Arabic homework.

"You are welcome," I was told, just like that. And hungry, I went along.

There was a silent dance that began when we entered the House of Curries, which seemed well rehearsed, and involved Dustin and Mohammad placing the large communal order at the counter, a few of the women—including Rasheeda and Faatimah Knight, another incoming Zaytuna College student—pulling water jugs from a small refrigerated case and moving them to tables on a veranda outside. All the while, the British student Zajif Iqbal, Ebad, and a few other men dragged over another table and a few additional chairs to accommodate everyone.

At dinner, I found myself seated across from Rasheeda and next to Faatimah, the impossibly composed eighteen-year-old from Flatbush, Brooklyn, who'd only just graduated from Brooklyn Latin high school, which had opened in 2006. Her parents were Caribbean, from the West Indies, she said. "I'm first-generation American and second-generation Muslim." We ate when the food arrived and she seemed to appreciate it when I told her I was somewhat ignorant about Islam. That's why I was there. She smiled. That's why she was here, too. "Isn't that why we go to school? To get over our ignorance?" Her father had taught her that.

Ebad left early to catch his flight home, and when I tried to pay my share for dinner the group refused to let me. I tried again. They refused again.

In his 2001 book *And God Knows the Soldiers: The Authoritative and Authoritarian in Islamic Discourses*, Islamic scholar and UCLA law professor Khaled Abou El Fadl writes, "Representing God's law to other human beings is truly an onerous burden. The burden is not simply to represent the evidence of God's particular injunctions, but to also internalize God's goodness and morality within oneself. The burden is one of diligence and honesty, not just with the textual sources, but with oneself—to bring the intellect and conscience to bear upon how we evaluate and understand the evidence."

This had always been Zaytuna's burden. In one form or another, the Arabic classes and some form of instruction in Islamic law and theology had been going on since the mid-1990s, when Sheikh Hamza returned from his studies in the Muslim world and began his public life with Zaytuna Institute. The classes and outings going on over this summer were somewhat old hat; the teachers knew what they were doing. Many of the students had returned for a second or third summer in a row. Several of Sheikh Hamza's and Imam Zaid's early students, for that matter, including Imam Dawood, the Ta'leef Collective's Usama Canon, and even Ebad, had also begun to take on the burden of "representing God's law to other human beings." When these summer classes ended, Dawood would be leaving the Bay and not returning to his New Haven congregation at Masjid al-Islam; he was taking a chaplain position at Dartmouth College, where he would also serve as the Muslim Life and Service Trips Co-ordinator for the William Jewett Tucker Foundation.

Yet for all its popularity and all it had accomplished to meet the needs of a growing local community with a deepening interest in tra-ditional Islam, Zaytuna Institute had always been a little ad hoc, its course often shaped by the rising and falling interests of the man at the middle. And while Sheikh Hamza's ideas had remained central to the development of the curriculum and philosophy of Zaytuna throughout its pilot seminary program and now as they prepared to welcome a first class into the nation's first Muslim college, other voices had in time become just as important. Imam Zaid had been the engine of the seminary program. Dr. Hatem Bazian would be the col-lege's third cofounder, a professor of Islamic Studies at UC Berkeley who'd been involved with Zaytuna from its earliest days—teaching Arabic, organizing the institute's yearly conference. His involvement became instrumental when the possibility of expanding Imam Zaid's seminary program in Hayward into a full college was brought to the table in 2007. Dr. Hatem insisted that their campus in Hayward was just too far-flung; a small liberal arts college would need a tighter geographical connection to other institutions of higher learning, in Stanford, say, or Santa Clara, San Jose, or Berkeley, which to Hatem had always seemed "the natural place, a hospitable city . . . with a critical, intellectual mass."

These kinds of core decisions, about whether the school would eventually become a liberal arts college or whether they'd be better off continuing as a seminary, whether they would relocate within the Bay or perhaps move to the city of a major funder, about what sort of Arabic they would teach and how much fluency they'd require for admission—all these decisions involved long, sometimes laborious debates. Some of them were still going on and would continue to throughout the year.

Most recently, Zaytuna had brought on Omar Nawaz, an operations expert with a technology background, whose most recent position had been with Microsoft. Born in Lahore, Pakistan, he still carried an accent from a hometown he remembered fondly—that "old walled city"—and which he compared to Jerusalem, a place he'd loved when given the chance to visit. Through the late '80s and early '90s, Omar had studied at Brigham Young University, where he read the Hebrew Bible, the New Testament, and of course the Book of Mormon, and later at the University of Utah, before becoming a product manager at Cisco Systems. He'd also founded a small tech company that sold software that offered parents control over their children's smart-phone activity. That product seems never to have made it out of the beta phase.

Omar has a round face and, when we first met at a coffee shop near the UC Berkeley campus, wore a tightly cropped goatee. He dressed in a dark gray suit and left the collar of his shirt open. We talked about his plans for the approach of Ramadan, how, while he hoped to be able to observe the rising of the new moon this year, in his experience it had often been difficult to make out when it corresponded with the setting sun. "Some people," he said, "are specially trained." Like Imam Zaid and the students on the hill, he looked forward to rising before dawn throughout the holy month to take advantage of the fast. There was a spiritual point to rising early enough to eat. Getting up before the sunrise required discipline. And though you would eat in the darkness and were expected to start the day full, whatever humility or longing or basic hunger a fast could provoke would start hours before most other people were awake, in the blue dark of the morning, and not end until the sun sneaked away for the night.

And the first light of dawn, he said, what he referred to as "one edge of the black whale"—the thinnest sliver of the sun—was always something he loved to show his kids.

Though hired to run the school's administration, and with just weeks before Zaytuna started classes, Nawaz still couldn't tell me certain things. First, he wasn't exactly sure how many students there would be—"definitely fourteen, though possibly sixteen." Omar also didn't know where the college's campus was; it hadn't been settled. He didn't know for certain; Sheikh Hamza didn't know; the students certainly didn't know. They were still in negotiations with a landlord.

This is what Omar did know: The school would offer two majors at first, Arabic and Islamic law and theology. At least this year and for the foreseeable future, students would move through their classes as a cohort. This first term, Imam Zaid would teach Islamic history from the seventh century to 1492 and also teach a section of law. Wednesdays, Sheikh Hamza would teach Introduction to Islamic Theology. Dr. Hatem would cover economics starting in January. Another member of the faculty who also taught Arabic in the summers, Abdullah bin Hamid Ali, would offer another section of law and also teach Arabic. Abdullah was called *ustadh*, or teacher. A Muslim professor from Ohlone College, Dr. Shirin Maskatia, had been brought on to teach English composition. And except for in the classroom for Intermediate Arabic I, English was the language of the college—another of those matters subject to ongoing internal negotiations.

Zaytunah is the Arabic word for "olives," a food that "must be treated by human hands in order to become palatable fruit," to employ a phrase the school's founders have used often over the years. "The process of curing olives," they continue, "has long been used as a metaphor for the maturing of the human heart." This is as true for Jews and Christians as it is for the Muslims. "Its oil," says the Koran, "[is] nearly luminous even without fire touching it."

Founded on the principle that in order to take root Islam must produce religious scholars in the lands where it moves, Zaytuna College means to make America a Muslim country—as much as it may be a Christian one. And what Omar could tell me the morning we met was that American students would make up the inaugural class. I would come to know these students. Among them were Faatimah and Mahassin and Sumaya, Haroon and Adnan and Abdul Jalil, Christopher and Dustin and Veronica. *Alhamdulillah.*

TWO

Al-Madrasah

Students have desks, and they're sitting on chairs, and the
faculty is teaching. So, all is well on the Western front.

—Hatem Bazian

Except for those who were joining Zaytuna's inaugural class, the summer Arabic students had mainly left by the time the college opened its
doors for a first public viewing. The convocation was slated to begin
at five thirty in the afternoon at Berkeley's International House, located at the foot of the Hills and the start of Bancroft Way. By now,
Monday, August 23, Ramadan had arrived. None of the Muslims had
eaten all day. *Iftar*, the evening meal to end the day's fast, was included
as the final item in the convocation's program.

While an audience slowly filtered in, I waited on the aisle about
three-quarters of the way back in the hall; Maryam Kashani, with her
camera, circulated near the stage, which was lined along the front
with votives and had a low table situated at its center, in front of
eight empty chairs. Sheikh Hamza Yusuf had wanted an occasion that
seemed both dignified and unpretentious. Tasteful, metal decorative
lamps hung on either side. There were autumn leaves and flowers.

The audience was surprisingly thin at the start—whole sections
of seating were empty—but the hall would fill in over the next twenty
minutes or so, even as the speeches got under way.

I'd arrived early, but not that early. We were operating on what
I would later hear referred to affectionately as "Muslim standard
time": most things start late and everything continues apace until
it's over. For a community whose attention is so regularly focused
on accurate reports of moon sightings and precisely timed prayers
five times per day, there is generally little concern with schedules.
Or, maybe it's truer to say that certain schedules—say, again, those
prayers—ruin the schedules of most everything else. Priorities. In

the coming months I'd more than once find myself waiting around Zaytuna's campus someplace—the kitchen, the foyer, on a bench in the quad—because someone, or just as often everyone, had to pray.

This day, following afternoon prayer, or *asr*, which, like *iftar*, had been scheduled into the ceremony, Veronica Hernandez, one of the school's incoming students, offered a recitation from the surah Maryam, named for the mother of the Prophet Jesus. Maryam, or Mary, is the only woman referred to by name in the whole of the Koran: "And mention Mary in the Book," Allah instructed the Prophet Muhammad. And so they would mention her here, as well.

Narrated in the passage they'd chosen for the convocation is a moment Christians would recognize as the miraculous conception of John the Baptist by Elizabeth, who in the Koran is known only as the wife of Zacharias. As for Maryam, her story sounds familiar, too: "How will I have a son," she says, "when no man has touched me and I have not been unchaste?" The reply: "Your Lord says, 'It is easy for Me; and We intend to make him a sign for humankind, and a mercy from Us.' So the matter is decided." Jesus was here today, too.

With Veronica leaving the stage, the faculty then stepped through the hall with swift confidence, the three founders, Dr. Hatem, Imam Zaid, and Sheikh Hamza, leading the way in black academic robes and satiny blue stoles marked at each end with a symbol of the Prophet's sandal. Sheikh Hamza would later tell the audience that these sandals, simplified and stylized over the centuries into a kind of emblem that you'll find on display in mosques and madrasahs and homes from Syria to India to Morocco, represented the competing emotions of fear and hope; this was an appropriate symbol today as they walked this college and its students into the world. But he'd also say that for Muslims everywhere, no matter the day, these two emotions and the memory of the Prophet were necessary to the path of Islam in general. The sandals at the ends of their stoles meant that on the one hand the founders feared their "intentions might not be up to the standard they need to be," or that Zaytuna might not be accepted by God as a place of sacred learning. On the other hand, with what they saw as such a bold venture, they hoped that they were truly trusting in God—and not simply themselves—in the first place. For

Sheikh Hamza specifically, the sandals of hope and fear were basically Dante's "paradise and inferno," a first reference I'd hear in my time with the sheikh to a "great books" tradition he hoped to bring to the school.

James Donahue, president of the Graduate Theological Union and the evening's keynote speaker, followed behind Sheikh Hamza in a red robe. Every one of them carried prepared remarks. Not everyone would rely on them.

Behind them came the students in a line, fifteen in all, six men and nine women, interspersed, from all over the country. The whole procession was accompanied by a recording of prayers chanted over the rhythm of drums.

Observing the proceedings from his place a few rows behind the students was Omar Nawaz, the operations expert, whose particular brand of intensity gave the impression that he could be both perched at the edge of his seat and sunk deeply into it at the same time. He draped an arm behind a seatmate.

Dr. Hatem handled all the introductions, moving back and forth from his seat to the podium. And James Donahue's keynote address, which he called "Ethics and Religious Institutions of Higher Education: Beginning the Journey," was preceded by the reading of an original poem, titled "Book," by Rasheeda Plenty, the woman I'd met on the hike who'd been on the fence about joining this first class. "Like people who have never seen trees," she read, "we stand gazing at our chests / to see what will come / of our bodies, / this strange planting here." This was a first reminder, probably unintentional, that *zaytunah* is the Arabic word for olives.

With his remarks, Donahue, a Catholic ethicist, offered Zaytuna both encouragement and a set of intellectual and practical requirements that would be part of finding their place in the world of American liberal arts. His address highlighted the ethical challenge Zaytuna faces to incorporate into its mission the value that American democracy places on rights and liberties, pluralism, pragmatism, democratic justice, and creative novelty. "Zaytuna," he said, "is an academic institution—a college. It is not a mosque; it is not a community center; it is not a gathering space for religious rituals; it is not a cultural center—although elements of each of these will surely be part of Zaytuna. The challenge for Zaytuna will be to determine in what ways it will serve the Islamic tradition and how it can enable that tradition both to preserve and grow." This would only happen, he concluded, through the care and attention the school gave its students. In practical terms, the challenges laid out by Donahue might be seen to correspond with the requirements for accreditation set forth by the Western Association of Schools and Colleges. As the association lays it out in its handbook, accreditation would require demonstrating a commitment to both "institutional capacity"—*Zaytuna is an academic institution*—and "educational effectiveness," which in general would require clarity of purpose, institutional integrity, fiscal stability, and the necessary organizational structures to carry out what WASC considers "clear and appropriate educational objectives and design at the institutional and program level." In taking its first steps toward independent accreditation, Zaytuna had made the decision and placed the bet that training in traditional Islam could clearly be seen—and judged appropriate—alongside any other academic training offered in the United States. In putting this in ethical terms aligned with American freedoms and rights, Donahue had effectively upped the ante.

The crowd was appreciative of Donahue, though not raucous in their reception. There was the sense that the speaker they were all waiting for was still to come.

Imam Zaid, working from written remarks that he said would keep him from wandering off, used his time to offer the students advice. It sounded simple: "Stand for, stand on, and defend the truth." On behalf of the founders, he said, "It is our fervent prayer and hope that the truth you students will write will flow from the pen of your hearts, for the heart when it is upright will always bring forth the truth." He then concluded with a reading from the Rudyard Kipling poem "If," offering as a caveat that it was "written by a person who is not one of my favorite poets." Kipling, Zaid said, had also written of "the white man's burden." During his reading of "If," Zaid doubled back at a point to repeat these lines, which seemed to hold special, personal meaning, and a particular meaning for a misunderstood American Muslim: "If you can bear to hear the truth you've spoken / Twisted by knaves to make a trap for fools, / Or watch the things you gave your life to, broken, / And stoop and build 'em up with worn-out tools."

Offering a reading by the British Muslim scholar Martin Lings was Virginia Gray Henry, an academic publisher from Louisville, Kentucky, and a direct descendant of the American revolutionary Patrick Henry. Henry stood wrapped in fabrics, peering out from Revolutionary era–style spectacles.

For the people who conceived of Zaytuna College, it seemed it wasn't so much what Henry might say on their stage, as what she, given her ancestry and her Islam, meant simply by being there. In his own remarks near the end of the ceremony, Sheikh Hamza was clear about what she meant to him: "I think it's auspicious—and I don't say this lightly—that a direct descendant of Patrick Henry is here with us in this convocation. Because he really started the American Revolution, and this is part of the American Revolution. What's happening here today is part of the American Revolution, because America began as a place that wanted to depart from the ways of the old world. And the way of the old world was fighting each other over religious doctrine. This was a place [where] they actually wanted to see people actually able to express their faith." And then, with a nod to the Prophet Muhammad in what appeared to be a Freudian slip, Sheikh Hamza added, "What was articulated in starting this revelation—revolution—was 'Give me liberty or give me death.'"

Beyond the subtle awareness that while on campus I might never have to open a door for myself and would have to insist on paying for my own meals, one of the most striking realizations I had after my first weeks around Zaytuna—and this might go for entering into any new, somewhat insular community—was that they indulged in a celebrity culture all their own. This was made all the more clear the first time I saw Hamza Yusuf in person: When Sheikh Hamza is in a room he absorbs all the stray attention. He's handsome and wears a dark goatee; he dresses sharply in long black coats and white shirts with open collars; he very often wears a kufi, but not always. And it's obvious that people watch him.

He is the one they wait for, the one everyone comes to hear. Listed among the attendees of an event, Sheikh Hamza always head-lines. The man can change the course of a fund-raising effort simply by wandering up onto the stage, taking a seat, and casually leaning back. Money pours in. In a world where most musical instruments are broadly forbidden—that is, *haram*, or sinful—it's somewhat surprising that he's often referred to as their "rock star." His horn-rimmed eyeglasses, which carry a slight blue tint, call to mind the cool distance behind Bob Dylan's Wayfarers as much as they pay tribute to the legacy of Malcolm X, which, at first glance, seems the more obvious point.

Taking the podium to offer his closing thoughts at the convocation, Sheikh Hamza praised Donahue for his remarks, making a point to note the toughness of this crowd—*no standing ovation!*—and proceeded to draw connections between the challenges to founding Muslim institutions and the struggle Catholics faced to establish themselves in this country. Both had to assert their rightful Americanness. His own family was Irish Catholic. Once known as the O'Hansons, they only later became the Hansons. Catholics, he said, were persecuted in Philadelphia, and churches were burned in 1844; his mother's family, Greek Orthodox Christians, was persecuted in San Francisco. His people built churches. What that generation had that this generation seems to be missing, he said, was dignity. And no matter how pleased and proud and hopeful they all were to be opening this college, the world out there often saddened him. "I don't know," he said, "how anybody could be happy about seeing young people with such a loss of dignity."

In a book Sheikh Hamza coauthored with Imam Zaid in 2008, *Agenda to Change Our Condition*, they made clear what they believed was possible within a Muslim school and perhaps no longer possible elsewhere. "Beautiful and inspiring *madrasah*s (schools)," they wrote, "where the love of Allah and His Prophet (PBUH) [meaning, "praise be upon him"] was instilled in the hearts of the students along with a rich understanding of the *deen* (religion) of Allah and with memorizations of His Book, have been replaced by hideous, secular institutions that instill in people a disdain for the past and a boredom that lingers long after the last empty book has been closed and an equally empty career begun."

Zaytuna, with its Islamic framework, would be different, because "religion," he said, "is about dignity." And though Hamza's tone during the convocation was generally more conciliatory than the one he and Imam Zaid had taken in *Agenda to Change Our Condition*—there was less talk of the hideousness of the secular world, say, but ample room for carping on the "global uniform" of T-shirts and shorts—instilling a sense of dignity in his students that they might not get elsewhere, from the way they dress to the way they study, would be from this moment at the very heart of what this college would set out to accomplish.

"That really is," he said, "what education is about." In other words, religion and education were really about the very same thing. And the example must be set from the top. First, do no harm. "We know what harm is caused by humiliating children," the sheikh continued, and then turned for a lesson to whom he called "the great articulator of Islam," the eleventh-century Persian philosopher and jurist al-Ghazzali, named by Zaytuna as "among our illustrious perennial faculty": "Never scold a child in front of other children, but always take it aside. Because when you shame a child in front of children you create humiliation in their hearts, and they will lose their sense of shame. They will get worse and worse." The Islam they were setting out to teach made it so that such a thing could not happen here.

Zaytuna, he admitted, was now just an "attempt," a kind of experiment whose success would be determined by the support of the community—and, of course, by trusting in God. The support, a word that included everything from prayers to large checks, to this point had been good, he added, but "nowhere near" what they would need. He had gotten everyone this far, in part on the sheer force of his will, and now those fifteen students were there, looking at him. Their parents were there. The community looked on. "This is a courageous group of young people. They really are. Religion is about faith and their presence here really is an act of faith." They'd placed their faith in him and Imam Zaid, and to a certain extent Dr. Hatem and Omar

Nawaz—the "boss man," as the students would come to call him—
the two pulling the many levers behind the scenes; they'd placed
their faith in them nearly as much as in Allah. And Sheikh Hamza
seemed genuinely humbled.

Sheikh Hamza loves the Robert Frost poem "The Fear of God."
He's committed it to memory—along with some Bob Dylan lyrics
and the Koran, both on display during his speech—and as he brought
the evening to its end, he recited it. It struck me as a moment of autobiography, or for the audience some sense of what Hamza Yusuf daily
reminds himself about his rise in the world. Frost's poem insists, "You
owe it to an arbitrary god."

This humility—the fear of Frost's arbitrary god—said Yusuf, was
"the great quality of the Prophet," who was commanded, he said, "to
be humble so that no one would show arrogance over any other." Tomorrow was the first day. He wished the crowd a blessed Ramadan.
He'd done this all without notes.

"I really hope that we set out humble with the task that is ahead.
It's an immense task." And of the students, he concluded, "I'm really
hoping that we can serve them as well as they're expecting us to."

Following the ceremony and before I even had a chance to learn
who I was talking to, Usama Canon offered to treat me to some re-
freshments from the café in the front of the International House. It
seemed someone had told him a friend of Ebad's had come to see
Zaytuna. He would never call me anything but Professor.

Maryam had told me when we reached the bottom of the Berkeley Hills about the beloved Canon, a convert and an early student of
Sheikh Hamza. The students, she'd said, loved the classes and youth
programming he ran out of Ta'leef Collective, especially his huge
Sunday-night celebrations of singing and poetry, drumming and
prayer. At Ta'leef they burned incense. They served mint tea in perfect, tiny, metal-rimmed glasses; kids who'd come with their parents
would walk it around on trays. Events lasted into the early morning.
Often Imam Zaid would arrive late and sit on a low step at the front
of the massive assembly hall, sometimes just to listen. And while the
women were separated from the men on either side of low, movable
bookshelves, as Canon explained it to me, the arrangement was ul-

timately up to them—the women. Tradition, of course, had its own thing to say. The sides of the room had separate entrances.

Ta'leef, he explained, was a community-outreach spin-off from the now defunct Zaytuna Institute, located in a business park about forty miles down along the bay, in Fremont. Their motto: "Come as you are to Islam as it is." Canon invited me to come down for a visit the following day; he would give me a tour of the facilities. Seeing me as a traveler, I suppose, he offered an open invitation to sleep there anytime I'd like; the classrooms were all outfitted with rugs and prayer mats. There was a bathroom down the hall. "Make yourself at home."

Despite what Sheikh Hamza and Imam Zaid have written about the "hideous, secular institutions" in the United States, neither of them advocates a retreat from the world. Among Zaytuna's stated goals is the development of a "theistic worldview as a basis for informed reflection and the reformation of the licentious elements permeating our culture." Note that this does not include a reform of Islam itself; as with Ta'leef Collective, coming to Zaytuna means coming to Islam as it is. The school's mission is to "educate and prepare morally committed professional, intellectual, and spiritual leaders who are grounded in the Islamic scholarly tradition and conversant with the cultural currents and critical ideas shaping modern society." Imam Zaid developed a piece of shorthand for this mission. Zaytuna brings together the text and the context: the Koran meets America.

So, unlike what we often find in the history of American Catholic and especially evangelical Christian colleges, which were very often founded in a spirit of retreat from the culture at large, from the outset Zaytuna was intent on taking an advance position relative to the culture. By no means always progressive, the founders are committed to what the Chicago-based scholar Dr. Umar Faruq Abd-Allah, a white convert whose embrace of Islam in 1970 was inspired by *The Autobiography of Malcolm X*, as much a product of American culture as anything else one can imagine, sees as a long tradition within Islamic civilization, lost on many contemporary Islamists, of "harmoniz[ing] indigenous forms of cultural expression with the universal norms of its sacred law." Taking up this claim in the 2004 essay "Islam and the Cultural Imperative," what Dr. Umar argues is that in China Islam looks and sounds Chinese. In India Islam is Indian. His travels around the world have borne this out. And his travels around America must be no different. At Zaytuna, Islam sounds like Robert Frost and Bob Dylan and Patrick Henry. Just as for the *ummah* anywhere else in the world, according to Dr. Umar, Islam requires the "development of a sound Muslim American cultural identity . . . resolutely undertaken as a conscious pursuit and one of our community's vital priorities. . . . Islam does not merely encourage but requires the creation of a successful indigenous Islamic culture in America and sets down sound parameters for its formation and growth." And insofar as Zaytuna brings those Islamic parameters to bear on a college education, which means situating God and the moral life at the center of education while finding the good in the principles of American liberal arts, they're doing exactly what the religion requires of them. As Dr. Umar concludes, "the Prophetic message was, from the outset, based on the distinction between what was good, beneficial, and authentically human in other cultures, while seeking to alter only what was clearly detrimental."

Zaytuna was founded largely to reflect the principle that Islam is not culturally predatory, and to help avoid what Dr. Umar sees as "the destructive impact of culturally predatory Islamist ideologies from abroad," especially with converts like himself, but particularly among the growing number of black converts—the majority of American-born Muslims. Those predatory ideologies include more literalist and ultraconservative approaches like Salafism and Wahhabism, brands of Islam also known for the militant minorities within them. For me, Dr. Umar's essay was an early introduction not just to the diversity of the Muslim American community but also to the ongoing and often fractious struggle for authority that works itself out in essays, public and recorded lectures, and the endless jockeying that goes on all over the Internet by leaders and followers alike. Celebrity follows knowledge in American Islam.

Of course, I'd gotten an early sense of just how celebrated these scholars were when Ebad wrote those glowing essays comparing Imam Zaid, someone I'd never heard of before, to the towering Malcolm X, who had made a pivotal move to traditional Islam near the end of his life and whose renown among America's traditional Muslims seems uncomplicated by his long affiliation with the black separatist Nation of Islam.

Usama Canon's star was rising in its own right, and his own admiration of Malcolm X and the lingering influence of the Nation of Islam were obvious in the sharp deliberateness of his outfits, his classic horn-rimmed glasses, and the occasional bowtie. When I visited Ta'leef Collective for the first time after meeting Usama following the Zaytuna convocation, it came as no surprise to find in the foyer Thulani Davis's *Malcolm X: The Great Photographs*, with Eve Arnold's profile shot of Malcolm wearing a black fedora and wristwatch, his hand gripping the back of his neck, and at the center of it all his trademark ruby ring, with a star and crescent. Also around the building were flyers announcing that Dr. Umar was slated to participate in a workshop and offer a lecture. Anticipation for that October visit to the Bay Area was already intense around Zaytuna, and when the day finally came, it would be celebrated with chanting and the rhythmic beating of a *daf*, a frame drum, outside the entrance to Ta'leef.

The first assignment for the students at Zaytuna was to read an essay by Dr. Umar, who has a standing and popularity in the community nearly as great as Sheikh Hamza's. This essay, published by Dr. Umar's Nawawi Foundation, a kind of storehouse for his scholarship, concerns innovation and creativity in Islam, controversial scholarly concepts debated over the centuries under the Arabic categories *bid'a*, which means "innovation," and *ijtihad*, or what Dr. Umar calls "critical legal thinking in search for answers to new problems."

When, a few days after the convocation, I found Dustin and another student, Haroon Imtiaz, at midday neither eating nor drinking at Mudrakers Café, a coffee shop owned (in part) by Dr. Hatem, Haroon had the essay flat on the table, opened to the second page. He'd not gotten far, having underlined words on the page and consulted the English dictionary for some of the more difficult ones. Though his parents are from Pakistan, Haroon's first language is English. Still, college words are different than high school words. And as he'd soon learn, words in Arabic would be a whole other story.

Dr. Umar's point in the essay is that both *bid'a* and *ijtihad* "are central to how we conceive of ourselves as Muslims, the types of practices we condone, and the future we envision."

Haroon, for one, seemed to be having a hard time at the start figuring out what the future might look like.

On September 8, NPR's *Morning Edition* aired a story by religion reporter Barbara Bradley Hagerty that when posted online was titled "New College Teaches Young American Muslims." Steve Inskeep introduced the report: "At a time when Americans are struggling with the question of where Muslims fit into this country, Zaytuna College has opened its doors in Berkeley, California. Happened two weeks ago. It is an American Muslim College—the first."

The school was open.

Hagerty met several of the students, including Faatimah, who passed on Smith College and Bard and the University of Chicago to attend Zaytuna; Adnan Alam, who admitted to feeling nervous about something happening at the school that might be "misconstrued" in such a way that people think, "Wow, these guys are crazy"; and, most unexpectedly, at least from Hagerty's perspective, Jamye Ford, a recent convert to Islam and Columbia University graduate who grew up in a very religious African Methodist Episcopal home in the American South.

When it opened, Zaytuna was a perfect story for National Public Radio. The AP was also covering it. I'd been driving with Dustin one afternoon while he fielded calls from Hagerty and a few other reporters. CD recordings of Imam Zaid's sermons and lectures had piled up on the floor of the passenger's seat. Dustin tossed a few in the back to make room for me.

Indeed, members of the media had already been talking about the college for months, even years. In July, during Zaytuna's summer Arabic course, a reporter for the San Francisco public radio station KQED's *California Report* aired a fairly sedate and straightforward story that emphasized Islam's flexibility in the context of America, the profound impact of the scholars on the students, the historical tradition of American religious colleges, and, indeed, some historical opposition to their establishment, especially against Catholic institutions.

When broadcast nationally the following day on NPR's *All Things Considered*, though, the report had been edited for a national audience in a way that made the school seem to be at the center of a controversy; Zaytuna's founding met fierce opposition in the shape of Fox News, whose commentary was taken from a report that aired in October 2009, when the network ran a segment posing this question about Zaytuna: "Educate or Indoctrinate?" So, the national NPR report that aired during the summer of 2010 and was posted online under the headline "Founders, Students Defend Islamic College" led with clips of the Fox anchors interviewing Frank Gaffney, president of the Center for Security Policy, a right-wing think tank. Once realized, Gaffney said in 2009, Zaytuna would represent a "stealth jihad in America," a phrase he would ultimately use three different times during his brief appearance on Fox. "Islam's insinuating itself into our academic institutions." Though none of the school's founders appeared on the Fox program in 2009, when NPR put the report together, Sheikh Hamza is quoted decrying state violence: "When you have states that bomb people, you're going to have people that are at the brunt of those bombs that are going to be very upset. Somehow, we legitimize state terror, and then vigilante terror is demonized." In the report, Dustin's temperature rises, too: "Islamophobia is so entrenched at this point in this country that for Muslims to do anything at this point, there's some level of defense that has to take place. But that's not to say that we should have to defend ourselves." In the story, even Zaid Shakir puts the founding of Zaytuna in the context of terror: "Because you see these foiled bomb plots, a lunatic fringe, and I think this is why Zaytuna College is so important. If we prove ourselves, even those more vocal critics will be silent. It's up to us. The ball is in our court."

Yet even while Fox was up in arms, a few months earlier and with a characteristically more evenhanded approach, the Associated Press had taken the occasion of a final June 2009 vote among Zaytuna's advisers about the viability of the four-year liberal arts program to report on the college. Gaffney wasn't quoted at all. "Jihad" and "indoctrination" seemed of little concern in the reporting. The founders maintained high, yet realistic, hopes: "It is a daunting task, there is no question about it," Dr. Hatem said. "But I'm completely confident and comforted that almost every major private university began with one classroom and possibly one building and sometimes it was a rented facility to begin with." Yes, Zaytuna would begin modestly. That said, even other Muslim scholars were not so convinced of Zaytuna's mission. Mahmoud Ayoub, for example, a retired professor of Islamic studies at Temple University, worried about the school's seeming insularity: "I don't know that I would send my child to go to a college where they can only learn tradition. Young people have to live," he said. "I like mixing people. I don't like ghettos."

A few months later, in late September, less than a year before the school would open, Laura Segall, writing in the *Chronicle of Higher Education*, focused her attention largely on the mounting challenges facing Zaytuna, particularly in terms of the money required to build, from the ground up, a college with aspirations to be an elite center of learning. (The founders would quickly become fond of reminding people while fund-raising that places like Harvard and Yale and Princeton all began as religious schools.) Though Imam Zaid and Sheikh Hamza spent much of the summer of 2009 "criss-crossing the country building support" for the college, mainly with events held in private homes, by the fall they were still "far from their goal," reported Segall, having raised perhaps 20 percent of their $5 million start-up budget. They had neither a development director nor a vice president of operations. And they had promised not to accept gifts from governments overseas. More ambitious fund-raising goals included between $15 and $20 million needed to establish themselves permanently in the Bay Area, and another $50 million toward an endowment.

Of course, given the state of the economy in the fall of 2009 and with a national unemployment rate creeping up toward 10 percent, Imam Zaid and Sheikh Hamza were often trying to tap drying wells; at the same time the ACLU had that summer released a report highlighting a precipitous decline in Muslim giving since 9/11, mainly the result of government investigations into Islamic charities and the "chilling" effect that had on potential donors: "The government's actions," the ACLU claimed, "have created a climate of fear that chills American Muslims' free and full exercise of their religion through charitable giving, or Zakat, one of the 'five pillars' of Islam and a religious obligation for all observant Muslims."

Where I live, little was said about Zaytuna's opening in the late summer of 2010. In New York, this was the season of Park51, known to some, mainly protesters, as the Ground Zero Mosque. The day following Barbara Bradley Hagerty's NPR report, Imam Zaid and Sheikh Hamza were once again on San Francisco public radio, this time discussing the opening of the college and, when the time came, reminding listeners that the proposed building project in New York City was neither a mosque nor was it at Ground Zero. In north Florida, a Christian pastor named Terry Jones had scheduled over those same weeks a day of Koran burnings to mark the anniversary of 9/11. Imam Zaid reminded listeners to KQED's *Forum:* "In normal times some guy in Gainesville, Florida, with a congregation of fifty or sixty people burning Korans wouldn't even be newsworthy." And though *Forum* host and religion writer Michael Krasny supposed that "most Americans" seem to believe that Islam sanctions the sort of violence that in turn inspires someone like Jones to destroy Korans, by Imam Zaid's reckoning, Jones's belief about Islam is "not indicative of any larger trends or attitudes. . . . But in this political climate we're in that's multiplied, amplified."

In the moment, Krasny, who in November would participate in a Zaytuna fund-raising event centered on the question of Muslim American allegiance to the nation, did not point out that Zaytuna had opened its doors to only fifteen students—less than a third the number of Jones's congregants.

Time's cover story the week the school opened asked, "Is America Islamophobic?" and focused on the "anti-mosque uproar." And though Zaytuna's opening was given the briefest of mentions in the piece—two lines, very near the end, after a reference to the first Muslim Miss USA—it came as further evidence that "most Muslims feel safer and freer in the US than anywhere else in the Western world." And it's true: except for complaints levied against the college in the comments section of several online articles about the school, for the most part in the weeks surrounding its opening Zaytuna had avoided any kind of protests whatever. Asked about this by Krasny, Sheikh Hamza said he thought it might have had something to do with the school's location. Since I'd first spoken with Omar Nawaz, Zaytuna had finally found a home, in a facility housing the American Baptist Seminary of the West, across the street from Berkeley's People's Park. "We're renting from the Baptists, too, by the way," he said. "And the biggest population next to us is the homeless population of Berkeley. So no one can say 'there goes the neighborhood.'"

THREE

Al-Tullab

Most of our youth who have grown up in this country cannot relate to the schisms that underlie many of our disputes.
They see themselves as Muslims, period.

—Imam Zaid Shakir

Knowledge is for the purpose of trying to craft a dignified
existence and an existence that is both individually and col-
lectively God-pleasing. That recognizes that life as we have
it is a gift. And that we are responsible for remunerating for
that gift. And knowledge is a means of perfecting the remu-
neration. Of paying a cosmic debt.

—Dr. Sherman Jackson

Leenah Safi looked forward to leaving her hometown of Ann Arbor,
Michigan, when she graduated high school. The daughter of Syrian
immigrants and the youngest member of Zaytuna's first class, Leenah
can't remember a time when she didn't know of Imam Zaid or Sheikh
Hamza. Whether attending annual Reviving the Islamic Spirit con-
ventions in Toronto or traveling to Chicago for yearly gatherings
of the Islamic Society of North America, for the Safis, appearances
by Zaid and Hamza made events like these family affairs. And the
scholars' influence on Leenah, even as a young girl, was enormous.
Because of them, she'd always felt Islam was bigger than it ever appeared to her in Ann Arbor.

Once the students, or *al-tullab*, had settled into a schedule of class
and study and prayer, and once the attention from the Associated
Press and National Public Radio died down, and once Ramadan had
come to a close, Leenah was the first Zaytunie to reach out with the
idea of arranging get-togethers where we could all meet and talk.
I'd explained in a few early conversations with her classmates that I

would be interested in such meetings as an opportunity to meet everyone and follow their progress over the year. They all knew I would be writing about them. So Leenah took the initiative and would organize a time and place, usually in the apartment the men shared above a Subway sandwich shop on Telegraph Avenue, and there would be hot tea and boxed cake and dried fruits to eat. Most of the women lived next door. Though they offered me a spot on a low couch, we all sat on the floor, shoes off.

In our first meeting, when we handled introductions, Leenah told me she had spent some time at a community college before Zaytuna offered her a "chance to get out of Michigan . . . and live in a different community." She'd never been able to find her place at the mosque, she said, which, compared with the community in the Bay, felt small and inhospitable. Just a little more than a month in to the first semester, Zaytuna was already proving a relief. Here there were welcoming and like-minded people—from the college to Oakland's Lighthouse Mosque to Ta'leef Collective—many with similar complaints about the communities they'd left behind.

There was, for one, Mahassin Muhsin, a petite, black woman from Trenton, New Jersey. She has a bright face and an easy smile, but is soft-spoken—such that at first I misheard her name and then referred to her as "Hasan," which is a man's name. My mistake got a laugh. As a girl, Mahassin had been homeschooled by her mother— "I played all day," she told me—and spent her teenage years at an Islamic boarding school in Brooklyn before dropping out. "I just stopped going." Like Leenah, Mahassin arrived at Zaytuna after some time at a community college, where she studied art and a little Chinese. Zaytuna, she said, already seemed "so much more welcoming" than her community in Trenton. And it was welcoming "to *everyone*, no matter who you are, or what you're doing." Not to give me the wrong first impression—that Zaytuna, for all its openness, was an anything-goes sort of place—Mahassin continued, "But they're also encouraging everyone to move toward a similar goal." In the classroom and in the mosque, the scholars were leading them toward what Mahassin called the "spiritual wholeness that everybody wants."

"At home," she said, "you have to be a certain type of person to be a part of the community—or else you get isolated."

Rasheeda Plenty, the poet I'd met the day of the hike, said that this sort of isolation is a problem she knew well from home, too. "At my community in Kansas City," she said, "there were some people, of course, it did work for. But personally, it didn't work for me. It didn't work for my sisters. My own mother, who teaches at an Islamic school, she's not part of the community. And she's been there for fourteen years." This results, of course, in the Muslim not wanting to go to the mosque at all because she believes she simply doesn't belong. "It ends up being completely fine if you don't go," Rasheeda said. "Why should I go? No one gives you salaams"—*As-salamu Alaikum*, the customary and much-beloved salutation of peace Muslims share with each other.

Haroon Imtiaz, whom I'd seen struggling with the students' first bit of reading for the semester, had the same problem in his hometown of Sterling Heights, Michigan, where most of his community is Indian or, like his family, Pakistani. "It gets even more complicated," he said, "when you have a community of similar people—then factions form, and people only say salaam to people they know." In Michigan, he said, "the community feels very subdivided."

Who knew that peace could be so divisive? At Zaytuna there are salaams around every corner, I said. So far, this looked to me like a community that was functioning. Wouldn't I find this someplace else? I asked.

Rasheeda answered, "You might not."

The inhospitality of the American mosque that the students were talking about that day has been the subject of much handwringing for leaders like Imam Zaid and Sheikh Hamza over the years. In his 2003 essay "Flight from the Masjid," originally published in Zaytuna Institute's now-defunct journal *Seasons*, Imam Zaid describes the mosque as "one of the noblest and most beneficial institutions in the history of humanity." (*Masjid* is the Arabic word for mosque.) And yet, "today in America, we find many Muslims who have either left, or were never fully involved in the life of the mosque." Listening to the group of Zaytunies that day, I had to ask, was it any wonder?

Back then, writing the year he joined Zaytuna as a scholar-in-residence, Imam Zaid complained that converts from other traditions were often put off mosques by the "confusion and repulsive physical condition that characterizes many of them. . . . One would be hard pressed," he said, "to find a church or synagogue with food smudged into the carpets, overflowing trash cans inside the sanctuary, devotional literature piled willy-nilly on the bookshelves, filthy bathrooms, and worship services disturbed by roving bands of unruly, undisciplined children." The children he refers to presumably represent the confusion converts encounter as opposed to something repulsive. That said, there was always at least one child roving his Oakland masjid each time I went to hear Imam Zaid preach, and no one seemed to mind.

A flight from the mosques was also the consequence, Zaid says, of their politicization, which results in sectarianism and the kinds of factions that Haroon complained about encountering back home in Sterling Heights. "We frequently hear terms," writes Zaid, "such as a Salafi mosque, an Ikhwani mosque, a Sufi mosque, and other such aberrations." Putting aside the great and complicated differences among these sects—though suffice it to say that the Salafis and Ikhwanis lean ultraconservative and activist and very occasionally militant, while Sufis are esoteric and mystical and generally pacifistic—there's meaning in what Zaid says here that resembles the first-century work of Saint Paul among the earliest Christians: "For it has been reported to me by Chloe's people," Paul writes to the church in Corinth, "that there is quarreling among you, my brothers. What I mean is that each one of you says, 'I follow Paul,' or 'I follow Apollos,' or 'I follow Cephas,' or 'I follow Christ'" (1 Cor. 1:11–12). Imam Zaid, like Saint Paul, would quiet all that sectarian noise: "When they become exclusionary appendages affixed to the mosque, they can be extremely alienating."

The way Haroon described it, his own immigrant community made Islam feel foreign, "very much the way it does in those people's home country." But ideas and practices that shape a religious life in Pakistan, he said, don't end up working out so well here. Still, none of this from Haroon, nor any of the others' complaints about their hometowns, seemed to put them off of those places generally or in the long term. Haroon was already talking about returning to Michigan with Zaytuna's vision of Islam for America—or, as he'd come to see it, Islam "how it is." Though exhibiting the vague enthusiasm symptomatic of his youth and newfound religious fervor, Haroon made the case for everyone: "We can send a real message out," he said, "go back to our communities. It'll spread around and we can make change."

Haroon's classmate Christopher Cusano, who had also been sitting with us in the men's apartment that day, told me this kind of excitement was something he'd often seen among Muslims. Such enthusiasm, Chris said, was very common in the days or weeks following an especially meaningful weekend seminar or all-day conference where an Islamic scholar travels to a community—in Chicago, say, or Toronto—to present on a specific piece of the shariah, the body of Islamic law, or maybe to raise funds for their brand-new Muslim college. "What the benefit tends to be is a temporary spiritual boost. It's motivation. But get one month away from that and there's probably little you've actually taken away from it." For Chris, Zaytuna represented "a totally different approach to how you teach people." The endeavor here was more like bringing up a child, the "developing, or rearing, of people," he said. And if that was the case, it didn't matter now that Haroon's ideas for change, or Muslim reform, were more or less without shape; they all had time, which at the moment was what mattered. Knowing Islam demanded it. By setting down roots in Berkeley, Imam Zaid and Sheikh Hamza had decided, Chris said, repeating Haroon's point though in a manner more moderate, "to develop certain people and send them back to the community instead of traveling themselves to those communities once a year." There was something practical, after all, going on here.

A twenty-eight-year-old white convert with a sharp red beard, Chris was originally from New Jersey but had arrived in Berkeley from Orlando, Florida, where he'd moved when he was thirteen. He'd graduated high school a decade ago and had since earned a bachelor's and a master's degree in political science from the University of Central Florida. He'd come to Islam, he said, in the summer of 2003; a friend had given him a Koran, the catalyst for his conversion, which was, as he put it, the final piece of "a lot of things coming together." He also studied for a time in the Middle East and did "a handful of things," including serving as the founding director of Orlando's Council on American-Islamic Relations (CAIR). Chris, who also sometimes went by the name Abdul Rahman, always carried a small digital audio recorder with him for lectures, which sat up on little legs like an insect.

The other students who gathered in October for the first of our regular get-togethers included thirty-five-year-old Clevelander Adnan Alam, a bear of a man, but like Mahassin Muhsin quite reserved at first. He had graduated from Cleveland State University with a degree in mathematics. His ancestry goes back to Pakistan, but his parents had lived in Uganda before immigrating to the United States during the rule of the dictator Idi Amin. After Adnan introduced himself that afternoon, he didn't say another word.

Though Sumaya Mehai, who wore more layers more loosely than the rest of the women, had always lived in California, moving between Santa Barbara and Los Angeles—it was "kind of a complicated story," she said—growing up she hadn't known of Zaytuna or the scholars. She'd only heard about the Zaytuna's Summer Arabic Intensive course three years earlier. Like Mahassin, she'd been home-schooled, but in her case it had lasted through high school. She'd been unfocused, she said, throughout her associate's degree in French and liberal arts at a community college, and was "definitely" feeling more focused here. Though she'd applied and had wanted at first to attend UC Santa Cruz, when her acceptance letter from Zaytuna arrived, "it wasn't really a decision anymore."

Of the students who got together that day, Hadeel Al-Hadidi, twenty-four, was the only one who didn't live with the others at the apartments near campus, a point of mild regret in terms of convenience and her friendships, but she really did like the privacy of living alone. Like Leenah and Haroon, Hadeel had moved from Michigan.

Her mother, who is very active in her local community and sits on the Board of Trustees at the masjid, is an American convert; her father is originally from Istanbul. Hadeel, a sometime radio deejay, had already earned an undergraduate degree in communications and a master's in electronic media, but her mother recommended the second bachelor's at Zaytuna as a way for her daughter to develop a deeper sense of her place in the community. She had told the Associated Press in September, "Zaytuna College is more of a personal thing, to make myself a better person, to better myself in my religion." That she was confronted with the AP at all was a surprise, though; arriving in August for the start of classes, Hadeel hadn't known the college was just getting under way. She had no reason to think she was news.

Over the first month, they'd all begun to adjust to long days of classes and their tendency to run overtime, "which is always enjoyable," added Sumaya. On Mondays, Arabic was first thing in the morning, followed by Sheikh Hamza's two-hour theology class. Then came jurisprudence, and after that history with Imam Zaid. The rest of the week—Monday through Thursday—followed a similar schedule, with an English composition class twice a week that had so far asked them to write about a favorite piece of literature and also about a "controversial issue." Flag burning was one possibility. Sumaya had written about what she called the "mosque controversy" in New York City. They had just started on a unit about capital punishment.

For Leenah and Haroon, in particular, adjusting to college itself had been a challenge. They'd never been taught to read with the kind of attention required by the scholars here. Like any college student around the country, learning to write long and organized essays demanded something new of them; so far, preparing for tests had required not only learning some very difficult material but also, and perhaps more fundamentally, coming to terms with how to study. "If we're all in the apartment," Leenah said, "all on our laptops, on YouTube or Facebook, it's difficult to study." True enough. For Haroon, the major obstacle he'd faced, beyond what was becoming a real struggle in Arabic, was learning to live on his own for the first time. "It's not like it's easy to devote all your time to your homework. It's a challenge." Imam Zaid wasn't making it easier. He'd offered extra credit—an extra evening class—for students who wanted to memorize pieces of *fiqh*, or jurisprudence.

A student lounge had recently been set up on campus with a few couches and tables and a small kitchen. The scholars had been encouraging them to study there. And yet even for those students who had come to Zaytuna with college degrees in hand, at Zaytuna, Rasheeda said, "the level of studying they expect from you is different." The others were of the same mind.

And one final thing they all seemed to agree on: When they came unprepared for class, they felt guilty. Which reminded them: Midterms were coming. They needed to study.

As I left, out came the books, and we all exchanged our salaams.

For its part, Zaytuna aspires to be the home of one of the richest Islamic research libraries in the West. And yet the collection would have to begin small, as with so much at the school, with books delivered over several months in boxes from Sheikh Hamza's and Imam Zaid's home libraries. For all of September and into October, the room designated to hold those books—along with an eight-hundred-year-old Koran and a four-hundred-year-old student notebook Zaytuna has in its collection, Omar Nawaz told me—was mainly used for storage. When I took my first walk around the campus building in October and saw the room filled with rolled-up rugs and boxes, I'd entirely mistaken it for permanent storage. It was also serving then as an occasional prayer room.

When I returned in November and first witnessed the room in any state that might properly be called a library, some books were arranged in shelves along one wall specifically, Arabic script running from spine to spine of individual collections, making a nice backdrop, Omar explained, for a lecture that evening by Dr. Sherman Jackson. Jackson, who is also known as Abdal Hakim, is an expert in the shariah and a prominent scholar in the community; at the time he was Arthur F. Thurnau Professor of Near Eastern Studies at the University of Michigan. (He has since moved to the University of

Southern California, where he was named the King Faisal Chair in Islamic Thought and Culture and Professor of Religion and American Studies and Ethnicity.) The lecture would be filmed, Omar said, and the library behind Jackson was meant to appear fuller than it actually was.

The $2.5 million campaign for 2010–11, which detailed costs for the campus lease from the American Baptist Seminary of the West, student housing, scholarships, and administrative wages, made no mention of putting together a first-class library. Phase II of the library project, looking ahead at 2011–12, had a projected budget of $30,000.

Before Dr. Jackson's lecture, I'd arranged with Leenah to meet again with the students. We would spend much of our time together talking about Islamic prayer and the life of the mosque.

To a certain degree, public prayer in Islam is a formal practice. The way a Catholic might know the appropriate moments to kneel in church or to make the sign of the cross with his right hand and not his left, the Muslim learns where to place her hands, and how to cross her arms during a prayer at the mosque. She learns when to stand and when to bend in supplication, when to touch her head to the floor. And unless you're specifically instructed in the subtle variations of movement during prayer, there's great potential for confusion, as is often the case with Catholics, too. "Prayer is not easy to learn," Sheikh Hamza has said. "Prayer actually takes effort." This is particularly true given the expectation at the mosque that you're not going to let your mind or eyes wander, which in practical terms means that you don't look around much at what other people are doing—a point Imam Zaid emphasized with characteristic good humor the first time I went to hear him preach during *jummah*, the weekly Muslim prayer service, one Friday afternoon at the Lighthouse Mosque. Offering a sermon that considered how "the state and the strength of the heart" is obvious on the faces of those around us, Zaid said, "Look at the face of the believers." And then with a generous smile and a laugh, he corrected himself: "Don't do it now . . . you're not supposed to look around in *jummah*. Do it after *jummah*. I can do it now. I can see all of you."

Having heard this same message at their hometown mosques—though I got the sense it was delivered without the same generosity—some of the students came to Zaytuna not only without a good sense of how to study, but also not really knowing how to pray. Until recently, several of them hadn't known there even was a right way to pray—much less that there might be right *ways*.

At her masjid in Brooklyn, for instance, where she'd been part of the congregation since before she could remember, Faatimah hadn't really ever felt like she knew what she was doing or, like Mahassin and Rasheeda in their hometowns, that she really belonged. "I prayed behind my father for years," she told me, which meant she'd tried to follow her father's lead. But then her older sisters began a practice that differed slightly from her father's, according to a different school of thought, which left Faatimah thinking, "Should I start putting my hands up here, or do I leave them down here like my dad?" Her conclusion: "You should learn how to pray before you start praying."

Leenah, too, picked up the specifics of formal prayer in bits and pieces from watching older people in her community in Ann Arbor. But she hadn't realized she'd never really learned how to pray until Imam Zaid, leading his class in Islamic law, set aside the text he was teaching from and simply demonstrated all the motions and, Leenah said, "really showed us how to pray."

In deciding to offer a major in theology and law, Zaytuna can't help but revel in the diversity of the tradition, which, where Sunnis are concerned—and Zaytuna was founded by Sunnis—approaches legal questions broadly according to four schools of thought, each considered the *madhhab* of a particular imam from the first centuries of Islam. At the start, Zaytuna had scholars to instruct in three of the four schools: Malaki, Shafii, Hanafi. (Missing was the Hanbali school of thought.) Imam Zaid was teaching jurisprudence, or *fiqh*—the interpretation of Islamic law, or the shariah, which has always been fundamentally inspired by the life of the Prophet—according to the Shafii school of thought, which was the practice of Leenah and Sumaya and Faatimah. Rasheeda was a Malaki.

For converts especially, it really is a matter of preference, and, for those who are even aware, not surprisingly often an arbitrary fact of your upbringing. "When I chose Shafii," Faatimah explained, "I didn't necessarily have all that good a reason. I asked my dad what he thought we were more accustomed to growing up." Her father insisted that although he hadn't followed a school of thought growing up, "he liked Shafii *fiqh*" and he "liked Imam Shafii." So they were Shafiis.

What distinguishes the four *madhhabs* are differences in the four great imams' readings of the Koran and the tradition of the *sunnah* and hadith, stories about the Prophet and his companions that were passed down in a more or less verifiable chain of transmission. In basic terms, the more verifiable the chain, the more authoritative the teaching. What must be understood about these schools of thought is that among Sunni Muslims—and as the *madhhabs* have been institutionalized within the Zaytuna curriculum—they are all considered equally authoritative, the interpretations of those early imams all equally valid.

During an event at UC Berkeley the previous day, delivering a lecture prior to the discussion he would lead at the Zaytuna library, Dr. Sherman Jackson had called this cultivation of diversity by Islam a "mercy." And one assumes he chose this word carefully. After all, mercy, "above other divine attributions," writes Dr. Umar, "is God's hallmark in creation and constitutes his primary relation to the world from its inception through eternity, in this world and the next." This essential pluralism is something that Islam shares with Judaism, Jackson said; both offer multiple ways of being one thing, different, yet equally valid ways, for instance, of conducting oneself in the public square.

That pluralism and intellectual ecumenism could themselves be a mercy—the most essential quality of God—is an idea that Leenah and Rasheeda had first heard from Sheikh Hamza and Imam Zaid. As Leenah said, "There's this amazing idea that if I'm in a situation and even though I generally practice according to a certain school of thought, in given circumstances I can borrow from another *madhhab*."

Meeting with the students, I couldn't help but see the rhetorical question take its obvious shape: Why do so many Muslims feel the need to see Islam as a narrow and needlessly wandering path when, as the scholars have shown them, it's wide and straight?

Of course, the even more obvious and immediate way that Zaytuna revealed to these students Islam's wide embrace of difference and diversity was the inaugural class itself, the scholars teaching from the front of the classroom or at the mosque, and the Bay Area Muslim community the students had just joined. As Haroon told me in an early meeting, "I think the reason here people are so welcoming is that it's so diverse. There's converts, there's blacks, whites, Pakistanis, Indians, people from everywhere. Where I'm from, my whole community is Indian and Pakistani. I'm just used to seeing those people. And if you have a white person walking into the mosque, you know, it's different. They might not feel welcome. Here it's different. They do feel welcome." Even I did, for the most part.

When he arrived that evening at Zaytuna following the *maghrib* prayer, scheduled for just after sunset, Dr. Jackson, wearing tweed and a white Nehru-style shirt, promised to offer his thoughts on the challenges and opportunities that Zaytuna faces in trying to bring traditional Islam inside the American academy. Presenting what he admitted were "some rather raw reflections"—further muddled, he supposed, by jet-lag—he spoke for an hour, first about the "friendliness" of the shariah to the "pre-Islamic" societies that the Muslims have entered into over the centuries, including the United States. Of course, Jackson's suggestion that America is currently pre-Islamic implies a time when the nation will be presently and properly so, which to these students and their teachers seemed both a hopeful and generally noncontroversial idea. I'd seen it more plainly stated by Imam Zaid. "Every Muslim who is honest would say, I would like to see America become a Muslim country," he told the *New York Times*'s Laurie Goodstein in 2006. "I think it would help people, and if I didn't believe that, I wouldn't be a Muslim." One important detail here is that he believes this should happen "not by violent means, but by persuasion."

As for Dr. Jackson, it was also not entirely clear that everyone in the room completely understood the implication of everything he was saying. Having heard him talk publically on three different occasions—once at New York's Jewish Theological Seminary, where, that night for the first time, I was required to pass through TSA-style security, and twice now in Berkeley—I'd begun to understand that there's a jargon that comes with his lectures, and a circuitousness and self-consciousness that can make him hard to follow. Sometimes even he's not quite sure what he's just said.

"Can you repeat that last part once again?" Chris Cusano asked at an early moment of Jackson's talk. Others in the room seemed to appreciate his asking.

Thinking back for a moment, Jackson replied, "I don't know."

What Jackson seemed ultimately to hope the students might take away was not a political message, but rather a practical one about balancing—even tempering—the Islamic tradition with an American scholarly tradition, and vice versa. With Islam as Zaytuna's point of departure, what can the students do to become what he called "critically confessional"? That is, how can they bring together their lives as students and scholars with their lives as Muslims? Catholics have been able to do it; so have Jews, he said. Although coming from Jackson it sounded almost purely academic, he warned that Zaytuna must come up with ways to avoid the traps of the liberal academy—presumably, at least in part, its comfort with atheism—while not forfeiting the academic training that he believes is required to critique liberalism. Elsewhere, that university education might be a sort of detour on the straight path of Islam. And yet, he knew as well the risk facing Muslims anywhere, even at Zaytuna: "The rewards of being able to speak in terms of the dominant reality are so seductive that the detour turns into the road."

Jackson's writing has mainly dealt with matters of race, particularly in the context of American Islam. And while, in his words, he got "a little bit gun-shy" bringing up race this evening, he used the experience of black Americans in this country to explain what he meant about the difference between a "dominant reality" and the minority one he's belonged to on at least two counts. "The advantage," he said, "to being black in this country is that the position presupposes having a kind of rationality that is different from the dominant culture." Why this is an advantage should be obvious. After all, where blacks are concerned, there have always been other ways of explaining American history and envisioning a collective future beyond those that have so far dominated. "If there were no other forms of rationality," said Jackson, "then I would be stuck with all that [the dominant] rationality has said about me." In this way, the American *ummah*, fully steeped in the tradition, has a lot to learn from American blacks. And it is so much the better when the person making this point is both Muslim and black.

Jackson, a true wanderer at heart, eventually brought his talk back around to the subject of *fiqh*, or Islamic jurisprudence, and where it ought to stand in relation to the academy. Given the central place Zaytuna had given to Islamic law and theology, Jackson's final points were of particular interest. And yet he seemed to worry he was once again moving into treacherous waters—although a survey of the room left me wondering why.

"I had no idea I'd be up here getting myself into so much trouble," he said.

"You're not in trouble," Sheikh Hamza answered from his seat in the front. "We're with you."

Beyond even the pluralism I talked about with the students, in a setting like Zaytuna, Jackson said, Islamic jurisprudence must be seen as flexible enough to engage with other scholarly disciplines. Highlighting two of his own disciplinary darlings, race theory and academic postmodernism, Jackson said, "there are certain high-placed individuals in the Muslim world who don't know anything." For the more practically minded American, he admitted that *fiqh* also seemed to have its limitations: "I don't know the position on single-payer health care, for instance." His point was that Islam, while always the point of departure (and presumably also the point of ultimate return), wasn't going to have every answer or provide every right approach. Good-faith engagement with ideas that are not necessarily Islamic must be part of the *ummah*'s "intellectual capital," Jackson insisted. That was his challenge to the students of Zaytuna.

For his entire talk, with each new point, Jackson had seemed somewhat on edge concerning what he was about to say. In the end, he explained, the whole while he'd meant simply to do no harm. "We are a community," he affirmed, "and we have done a lot of damage to one another over the years in the ways in which we've articulated some of these things. And I personally don't want to be a part of anything like that. Enough already, all right?"

FOUR

A Muslim Stillness

Wee shall shame the faces of many of gods worthy servants,
and cause their prayers to be turned into Cursses upon us
till wee be consumed out of the good land whether wee are
going.

      —John Winthrop, aboard the *Arbella*, 1630

I think people need more quietude in their lives; they need
more remembrance of God.

      —Sheikh Hamza Yusuf, 2007

On November 15, the morning I first finally visited Sheikh Hamza's
theology class, the room was overstuffed, even bursting, a fact made
all the more obvious by some unseasonable fall temperatures. The
students were all there. Others standing against the walls included
Zaytuna's staff—the administrator, Sadaf Khan, an editor, Najeeb,
even the "boss man," Omar, and several others—who sometimes
would take advantage of their closeness to Sheikh Hamza by auditing
the class, as it were. The rest of what filled the room, which is not
huge, mind you, one could call enthusiasm, and a good portion of it
was the sheikh's. Many of the students still actually seemed a little
stunned, or starstruck.

During my previous visit in October, around the time the college's phones arrived, I'd caught Hamza rushing from his car through
the entryway of the college on his way to the same class, the only one
he was teaching the first term. But after a month of media intrusion
following the opening of the school, most everyone around Zaytuna
seemed a little wary of my sitting in on his class then. I was told it
wasn't fair to the students. No matter that few of them seemed to
mind my being there.

When he arrived that October morning, I'd been catching up after Arabic class with a group of students, including Dustin and Haroon, who both scattered when they saw Hamza's car pull up around back—his wife, Liliana, a Mexican American convert, was driving. He burst out, briefcase in hand. If Sheikh Hamza had reason to rush so did they, and so off they went. Hamza paused very briefly to shake my hand and agreed to meet later in the day, if he could find the time. He was rushing to teach now and working on a translation, he said, and with the breeze that followed him in through the college doors, you got the sense he never stopped rushing.

I cannot be certain he even got my name that morning. We did not meet later that day. In fact, it would be months before Hamza found any real time to spend with me, and even then it was time we spent rushing.

That November day, I started early with most of the students in Arabic class. The teacher, or *ustadh*, Abdullah bin Hamid Ali, opened class with a prayer sung in Arabic. Roommates Haroon and Chris walked in a little late and took what seemed to be their regular place at a table near the window looking out onto Hillegass Avenue; Haroon still didn't have the required textbook. Ustadh Abdullah was going over the formation of ordinal numbers—first, second, third, and so on—and then moved on to a discussion of how, in Arabic, you can indicate that one thing is behind another thing. The whiteboard was, to my eyes, a wonderful and growing mess of squiggles and dots.

After a little more than an hour, following lessons in saying that someone is responsible for the earth and Abdullah's telling of an odd Moroccan proverb about the positive relationship between cheating and success, Chris asked a few specific questions about how to form some letters and most everyone else filtered out. Adnan turned in some homework; new homework was due Thursday, Abdullah said.

Sumaya got up from her chair front and center, spritzed the board, and then wiped it down. This same room had to be ready for Sheikh Hamza.

Prior to Hamza's class, the administrative assistant Ali Malik situated me nearly out of sight in the doorway of a small foyer off the back of the classroom, where the AV guy Haroon Sellars would film Hamza's discussion about atheist writer Sam Harris's best-selling *The End of Faith*. Sellars films just about everything, he's told me, for what are known as the Hamza Yusuf Archives. There's never any telling what Sheikh Hamza will say or when he'll say it. One moment from this particular class, with Hamza leaning back in his chair, explaining that Harris would have Allah—and Yahweh, too—go the way of Zeus and Apollo, would appear in promotional fund-raising materials for the school.

While Muslims around the world often gather in the thousands and tens of thousands for the sheikh's keynote lectures, Zaytuna's students have this front-row seat each week, which has made them the envy of their friends and families back home. Their Facebook profiles explode with quotations from their classes and videos of Sheikh Hamza—followed with comments: "Just looking at his luminous face made me smile:) May Allah (SWT) preserve him!" ("SWT" is an abbreviation for *Subhanahu wa ta'ala*, an Arabic expression meaning "may He be glorified and exalted.")

Over the past few days, and then in some last-minute cramming before the morning's Arabic lesson, I'd watched the students paging through Harris's book, which has a particularly tough assessment of where "we" stand with regard to the Muslims: "We are at war with Islam. It may not serve our immediate foreign policy objectives for our political leaders to openly acknowledge this fact, but it is unambiguously so." I'd seen underlining on the opening page: "The young man boards the bus as it leaves the terminal. He wears an overcoat. Beneath his overcoat, he is wearing a bomb. His pockets are filled with nails, ball bearings, and rat poison. The bus is crowded and headed for the heart of the city."

Having taught *The End of Faith* myself in religion classes at NYU, I'm well aware that in Harris's account the bomb soon goes off, and "all has gone according to plan." We're at war with Islam because Muslims are terrorists.

"Why is it so easy," Harris concludes, "so trivially easy—you-could-almost-bet-your-life-on-it easy—to guess the young man's religion?"

He's right, of course. Even here, at the buzzing center of Zaytuna, no one doubts that this young man Harris describes is a Muslim.

No one, that is, but Sheikh Hamza. If you take Yusuf at his word, for him it's not quite so easy. Although with Hamza there's always the possibility that he's trying hard—sometimes pushing the limits of credulity—to make a point.

"I wanted to say he was a Tamil Hindu! But we don't think of this because of oil!"

Dustin Craun piped up: "Most of Harris's book wouldn't be published in a good *newspaper*. It's unfounded, ridiculous." Having already been through one undergraduate degree, Dustin was more inclined than most of the other students to push back and argue with his teachers in the early days of the semester.

Still, unwilling to dismiss Harris's assumptions about Islam out of hand, Hamza wouldn't go quite so far so fast. *The End of Faith* isn't entirely unfounded.

In and out of the classroom, Sheikh Hamza is far from blind to the troubles facing the Muslim world or to the real threats of Islamic radicalism. In some ways, his authority in the Muslim world is rooted in the way he argues against Islamic violence and in favor of Islamic mercy—and always in defense of the shariah. This is the core of his teaching. "How do you feel about what Sam Harris says about Islam?" he asked. "He's not basing it on *nothing*."

This is where Hamza starts, with the *not-nothing* of Islamic radicalism. And his problem with America is that it's usually where we end.

Occasionally we locate a "moderate" voice to counter the extremists and call it a day. Yet, this simply can't be the case with Sheikh Hamza, whose commitment to the law and passion for the Prophet could hardly be described as moderate. So-called moderate Muslims also tend to be politically progressive, despite what traditional Islam might say about homosexuality or what a conservative like Hamza might believe about teaching evolution in schools. If we're honest about the growing numbers of Muslims in this country, and the growing influence of traditional, conservative Muslims like Hamza, "moderate" is not a broadly useful term to describe American Islam as it exists within the walls of Zaytuna. Because while the sheikh wouldn't claim to speak for all of America's Muslims—he's the first to remind you of the diversity of the believers, including the majority of American Muslims who almost never attend the mosque—he's clearly leading many, many of them somewhere. Into the Koran. Into the madrasah. Into the mosque and the public square. Which means that, ultimately, he's leading his students in the classroom and his followers throughout the country into America.

And so the class begins, and like so many of Hamza's addresses around the world, it is far reaching—touching on Mideast land disputes, Mark Twain's travel literature, Fox News's "media-created context" for Islamophobia, the politics of water in Kashmir, and even his "great-grandfather's death in the last battle of the American Civil War." Hamza Yusuf is known to be fond of this sort of free association, yet, as he was born in 1960, on this last point he probably meant to say his great-great-grandfather, whom we have to assume was one of only four soldiers killed at the Battle of Palmito Ranch, more than a month after Lee's surrender at Appomattox. He sprinkles his lectures with Arabic, which many of the students still struggle to understand. For him, it's second nature.

Hamza Yusuf Hanson, born Mark Hanson into a Catholic and Greek Orthodox family in Washington State, rose to national prominence in the wake of 9/11, when he was invited to the White House as an adviser to President George W. Bush. He's said to have convinced the president that naming the impending military operations in Afghanistan "Operation Infinite Justice" would offend Muslims, for whom the only source of infinite justice is God. Bush went with "Operation Enduring Freedom" instead.

In parts of the Muslim world, this meeting with the president earned Hamza the nickname "Bush's pet Muslim"; the sheikh's advice seemed to some to ignore the way the war itself, no matter the name, might otherwise offend—indeed, kill—his fellow Muslims. In his own defense, Hamza Yusuf would later claim, "Look, they call me the adviser to the president, but he didn't take my advice. I told him not to bomb Afghanistan."

Much has been said by critics everywhere—right, left, and center—concerning Hamza's ideas about America's position in the world and the nation's "war on terror." Some point to a speech in the days

before 9/11 in which Sheikh Hamza anticipated a "great tribulation" coming to America. Those critics might not acknowledge that
Hamza was, in his way, participating in a proud tradition of American
jeremiad that dates back to sermons delivered throughout early Puri-
tan New England, and was perfected during the Great Awakening by
Jonathan Edwards; more recently, one recalls the speech Dr. Martin
Luther King Jr. was preparing in the days before he was killed: "Why
America May Go to Hell." Hamza also likes to remind his critics of
a lecture he delivered in Philadelphia the day before this notorious
speech, in which he admonished the audience that anyone living in
this country or here on a visa acts against Islam when they undermine
the security of this nation. Rooted in a vague, uncomfortable feeling
that had been dogging him since August, and, as he has said, not
something he would ever *want* for his nation, the prediction of America's "great tribulation" brought the FBI to his house the very morning he met with the president. His wife, Liliana, sent them away.

On the other hand, there are also Muslim critics who still consider him a Western patsy and complain that the sheikh's not always
wearing a kufi. These days, though, during interviews and debates
about terrorism and radical Islam, he's still most often presented as
a "moderate" or "progressive" Muslim. When the *Times*'s Laurie
Goodstein reported on Hamza and his Zaytuna Institute in 2006,
she described him as sounding like "someone who is coming from
the political left," which position, she continues, "coming from the
mouth of someone who is unashamedly Muslim[,] can come across as
sounding very militant and very scary."

And yet, though Sheikh Hamza has come out as an unwaver-
ing and continually vocal opponent of Islamic terrorism—you hear
it even in the theology classroom—he's simply not what one would
call a "moderate" in the way that Muslim writer Reza Aslan, popular
author of *No God but God* and *How to Win a Cosmic War*, is often described. (Aslan is a regular on *The Daily Show*, something you wouldn't
expect of Hamza Yusuf.) Although, as Ebad has told me, it's true that
"balance, or being in the middle or moderation . . . is of course desir-
able in Islam," and that "preachers will often quote the verse which

is right in the middle of the longest chapter in the Koran (verse 134 of 286 verses), 'and thus we have made you a community in the middle,'" the kind of "moderates" that have gained a strong foothold in America aren't typically starting Islamic colleges from the ground up; they tend to enroll in centers for religious or Islamic studies at solidly secular institutions like the University of California at Berkeley (or, in Aslan's case, UC Santa Barbara). And despite what Goodstein has reported, "progressive" doesn't always seem quite right either. For instance, here's Sheikh Hamza advising Muslims on public education: "We must raise our children outside of the modern state schools that are designed to make them no more than functional literates. We absolutely must remove our children from state schools." (He and two of his siblings, one also a convert, work together on a Muslim homeschooling initiative in San Ramon, California, called Kinza Academy, founded by his sister Nabila and named for her daughter.) You can often hear a little of the libertarian in Hamza Yusuf: "Government," he's written, "is now encroaching on every aspect of our lives."

Another thing that separates Hamza Yusuf from moderates like Reza Aslan, whose first book was a best-selling call for a Muslim Reformation, is that he doesn't advocate for organized Islamic reform. All that Muslims need is already here—in the Koran, the shariah, and the centuries of scholarship Zaytuna has begun tapping into. Indeed, asked by Al-Jazeera's Riz Khan whether "popular and socially oriented movements like Hezbollah or Hamas are the beginning of a new, democratic and more progressive Islam," Yusuf responded: "Personally, I think we need a Muslim stillness rather than a Muslim movement. I think there's too much movement out there. We're living in times of incredible turmoil and I think people need more quietude in their lives. They need more remembrance of God."

This attitude may also account for why Sheikh Hamza has grown so popular among American Muslims and remains hardly known at all outside of the community. It's not reform he's calling for, but remembrance. And most Americans, knowing little about Islam, have nothing to remember—except 9/11, an event whose significance is wrapped in an entirely different sort of remembrance: Never forget.

. . .

In April 2008 Sheikh Hamza participated in a wide-ranging public conversation with Temple University's Khalid Blankinship about Muslim American citizenship, at New York City's Cooper Union—where, Hamza was quick to point out, Lincoln, too, once famously spoke. So had Senator Barack Obama just the previous month, campaigning on the promise to "renew the American economy."

Presented before a largely Muslim audience, much of Sheikh Hamza's talk addressed the Muslim's moral obligation to take part in the great American tradition of civil disobedience and the "sacred right" of dissent. Here he cited Thoreau and Martin Luther King Jr. and described civil disobedience as "the essence of Islam."

Asked during a Q&A about what advantages there are today to being Muslim in America as opposed to in a Muslim-majority country, he seemed to delight in the simple fact that in the thirty-odd years he's been a Muslim, there's never been more interest in tradition (for good and bad, of course). On the one hand, Yusuf seemed pleased with the very fact of a recent article that he'd read in the *New York Times Magazine* by Harvard law professor Noah Feldman, on the topic of the shariah; he likewise praised the article's fair-minded approach to what Feldman calls the "radioactive" subject of Islamic law, which also happens to be one of Zaytuna College's two majors. (Like Blankinship, Feldman has joined Hamza Yusuf in public conversation, Feldman's about the so-called clash of civilizations between Islam and the West.)

Though Sheikh Hamza refrained from saying more about the piece from the *Times Magazine*, Feldman's article, adapted from his book *The Fall and Rise of the Islamic State*, gives us an instructive way to consider the sheikh and the productive nostalgia that seems to animate so much of what he and the other founders of Zaytuna have set out to do. While Feldman's book deals mainly with his own hope, back in 2008, for a "gradualist constitutional change" led by democratic Islamists throughout the Muslim world—as opposed to the largely secular revolutionary movements we saw throughout much of 2011—what he writes about the "exalted status as keepers of the law" that Muslim scholars traditionally possessed, helps us see what someone like Sheikh Hamza and his colleagues might be attempting in this country.[1] While across the Muslim world there seems to be, as Feldman puts it, "little interest in restoring the scholars to their old role as the constitutional balance to the executive," in America, where there is no realistic hope for the creation of an Islamic state and where each Muslim is obliged by something like a contractual agreement to live as "an excellent citizen in the society"—a lesson Hamza once translated during a lecture by his beloved Mauritanian teacher, Sheikh Abdullah bin Bayyah—scholarship itself, and not politics, has become the cornerstone of Muslim leadership and the chosen path toward authority. (Writing about the Fort Hood shooting, Imam Zaid made a similar point: "There are no teachings from the normative corpus of Muslim political writings that allow a Muslim to violate the security of the public square, to endanger the lives of the general public, to attack non-combatant civilians, even in a battlefield situation, or to aggress against soldiers who are not in a battlefield. This is especially true where Muslims have entered into an explicit or implicit covenant of protection from non-Muslim political authorities and constitute a distinct minority in a particular land.") And so, where specifically Islamic executive or legislative national authority is not in the offing, American Muslims can do their best, most Islamic work, by participating in a proud tradition of interpretation and debate over, yes, the shariah. On this point, Haroon Moghul, an increasingly influential Muslim writer and lecturer on the shariah, has drawn this distinction (in a post to his followers on Facebook): "Sayings of the Prophet Muhammad, peace be upon him, are ethical guidance; they are not in and of themselves arguments.

---

[1]And to be clear, while Feldman's arguments following the 2011 Arab Spring draw appropriate attention to the mainly secular revolutionaries that toppled the autocrats of Tunisia and Egypt, for example, ultimately, he contends, the upshot of the movements was the inevitable and unequivocal victory for the Islamists. And good, he says: "Combining pragmatism and principle, mainstream political Islam has undergone an extraordinary democratic transformation. And it has done so in the very years when radical jihadism threatened Islamic democrats with condemnation and murder. From the standpoint of the global ideal of democracy, this is a victory of historic proportions."

Our tradition developed its vision of Islam by engaging all of the sources methodically, rigorously, and reasonably; to throw around hadith and use them to claim a conclusive argument is to miss the point entirely . . . [and] to do a tremendous disservice to our law and our philosophy." How much any Muslim can know with certainty about the law is a topic that generates a good deal of debate in the community; and in the end, even remarks that seem filled with certainty are suspect. The Muslims would tell you, *Allahu alam.* God knows best.

Whatever anxieties "the spread of the shariah" might generate outside the *ummah*, by Hamza Yusuf's telling they are absurd and ill-founded. As he sees it, the only piece of the shariah that may, in fact, cause some problems is a very small portion of legal rulings known as *al-ahkam al-sultania*, which, though it "gets all the emphasis," relates specifically to Islamic states and governments and things like penal codes. "It actually has no application whatsoever," he's said, "for normal Muslims." Not "normal Muslims" in the United States, at least. Yet, if the Islamists have their way throughout the Muslim-majority countries Feldman writes about—Egypt, say, or Libya and Tunisia—the *al-ahkam al-sultania*, he argues, might operate on the same basis it did under classical Islamic law, "combin[ing] extremely harsh punishments with a high standard of proof"—a standard that is, in most cases, prohibitively expensive and, as Sheikh Hamza has suggested, "a legal fiction."

Defenders of Islam's approach even to corporal punishment are fond of pointing out that applying the shariah in the case of adultery, say, as Hamza put it on public radio, requires "four witnesses"—men of good character—"that actually see penetration, and outside of a pornographic film I just don't see how that would be possible." That high standard of proof, in Hamza's mind, points to the mercy at the heart of Islam, where the role of the scholar has traditionally been to find ways around implementing whatever harsh punishments the shariah might call for. As Hamza sees it, that same impulse ought to shape Islam today, as well. "That should be the impulse," he's told me, "if your religion's based on mercy: How do we get around this?" By "this" he was referring to the punishment of stoning. Hamza would also remind us of a similar scholarly activity famous among Jewish rabbis, who have for centuries been devising loopholes and work-arounds when it comes to any number of difficult and outdated portions of the halakha, the body of Jewish law, including brutal forms of corporal punishment. "They've somehow been able to deal with those problems," he claimed, "but they don't *deny* stoning." They just don't stone people anymore.

In any case, what Feldman's account of Islamists throughout the Muslim world shares with Zaytuna's approach to the shariah is a nostalgic concern for Islam before both the militant extremists, who, they argue, have warped Islam by making out of it a "cult of death," and the brutal, typically secular autocrats who may have given Islam lip-service but just as often ignored its central concern for the rule of law.

If Feldman is right, and strange as this may sound to American ears, returning the shariah to its proper place in Muslim-majority states may depend on the election of Islamic democrats and their legitimate and successful governance—to say nothing of the rest of the world, most importantly, perhaps, the United States, allowing for such self-determination and self-government. For Sheikh Hamza, Imam Zaid, Hatem Bazian, and their American students, who all operate with the understanding that "Islam has never become rooted in a particular land until that land began producing its own religious scholars," returning the shariah to its proper place begins in classes in Islamic jurisprudence, or *fiqh*, and depends on their success as a school and the success of every other Islamic school that follows their lead.

Publically Sheikh Hamza very often relies on personal anecdotes and pieces of family history to provide color to a lecture or root himself and his Islam deeply in the American story (usually both). So, for instance, writing in the *Christian Science Monitor* about the "storm of emotion" during September 2010 around the plans for the Park51 Islamic center, he took lessons from anti-Catholic bigotry of the mid-nineteenth century, specifically the 1844 Nativist riots in Philadelphia, new home to his great-great-grandparents Michael O'Hanson and his wife, Brigid, who had only recently landed there after fleeing famine in Ireland. His great-grandfather, also Michael, dropped the "O" sometime in the years that followed, "hid[ing] his Irish ancestry even from his own children, to spare them the perceived shame of being Irish in upper class society," and eventually made his name, as it were, in newspapers both in Philadelphia and later Duluth, Minnesota. Name-changes notwithstanding, the upshot, which Hamza repeated with typical wordplay in lectures over these same weeks and months, is that over time "sense prevailed over sensibility," emotions calmed, and the newly American Irish "pressed on." Today, "Muslims are the new Irish," whose narrative "is also one of good cheer for the Muslims." "Slowly, they built some of the finest schools and colleges in our nation."

Like an off-the-cuff mention in the classroom of a great-great-grandfather's death in the American Civil War, this is an example of Hamza's penchant for blending family history with our larger national story. His family helped shape this country early on, and over the last half-century they have likewise reshaped it. After all, Hamza is very fond of pointing out that a 1964 photograph taken during protests of the Republican National Convention in San Francisco that shows his mother Elizabeth with a sign that reads "Civil Rights Is the Issue" appeared in an encyclopedia yearbook the following year. With Zaytuna—and even his sister Nabila's Kinza Academy—his generation of Hansons will do their part to shape this nation and its future. He believes in what he sees as the American way, which recognizes the fundamental equality of all people and codifies the right to practice whatever religion one chooses; and more, Hamza sees the very best of America modeled in the life and vision of the Prophet: "America . . . is the best model that we have to have a multifaith, multicultural society. It really is. In many ways, the Islamic civilization was a precursor to that, because there was a lot of conviviality in the Muslim world. . . . The idea of peoples living together is really an Islamic thing." The shariah, he argues, did not establish a specific form of government. Democracy, of course, is not laid out in the Koran. Hamza believes that Islam did, however, bring with it "con-stitutional' principles" that are radically egalitarian and merciful, including, he's written, "the idea of equality among races and gender, the concept of economic justice, and the right of an individual to be protected in his person and property from unjust search or seizure."

Given the shared focus on American and Islamic history that shapes Hamza's thinking about the institution he's helped found—and previous incarnations of Zaytuna were more specifically the product of Hamza's imagination—it should come as no surprise that his own self-image and claims to authority are based on what one biographer, Emory University Islamic studies professor Scott Kugle, has called the "precedence of the past." Of all the biographical sketches produced of Sheikh Hamza over the past decade, the one he considers most accurate—truest to his own sense of self—is Kugle's, which relies on a comparison between Hamza and the fifteenth-century Sufi jurist and reformer Sheikh Ahmad Zarruq. Kugle's book, *Rebel between Spirit and Law*, looks back to late-medieval Morocco to draw both a direct line of influence and a series of flattering comparisons between Zarruq and Yusuf that are meant to reveal as much about Yusuf's claims on authority as they do about those of his predecessor. (For his part, Kugle is probably most well known for his writings on homosexuality and Islam.)

The most profound effect Zarruq has had on Sheikh Hamza's career, especially since 9/11, has been in the way invoking this classical Moroccan jurist has allowed a modern American Muslim to develop as a spiritual leader and Sufi—though Hamza himself is cautious with this label, as Kugle tells us, fearing that he'll be seen as "cultish" if he goes around calling himself a "Sufi"—and at the same time position himself as a staunch critic of the puritanical and sometimes violent Wahhabis and Salafis. By and large, these Muslims, Kugle says, have shown themselves to lack both the "self-restraint and self-reflection" necessary for Islamic ethics and have "rejected not only Sufism but also Islamic legal reasoning."

Zaytuna, which I've seen referred to as a "Sufi seminary," has always been Hamza's effort to bring together the devotional quality you find in Sufis with the legal reasoning of scholars at a classical madrasah. Constraining its reach—Zaytuna cannot be all things to all people, they've realized in recent years—has been the result of both reflection and restraint. In this way, inviting only fifteen students the

first year could be seen as an exercise in Islamic ethics. And by balancing "law, Sufism, and humanist intellectual rigor," as Kugle says
Zaytuna has been established to do, "Hamza Yusuf is an active player
in the battle being waged over the character of the Islamic message."

But for Kugle, making the comparison between Hamza Yusuf
and Ahmad Zarruq doesn't end with each sheikh's effort to create balance between Islamic scholarship and devotion. Nor does it end with
their respective critiques of the worst elements of Islam. Nor even their
conservatism in the face of various revolutionary movements of their
times. The deeper connection Kugle sees is their common religious
authority as living saints.

Unlike in Christianity, say, Islamic sainthood is a status or distinction conferred on the living. Saints live a life apart, an exemplary life,
in many ways; they "confront the sacred," as Kugle explains. Having
done so, the saint assumes a new and onerous responsibility of offering
others access to the sacred as he confronts it. This makes them very
popular, as you might expect. But that's not all, says Kugle, because

> saints are controversial; they hover between the murk of routine
> personhood and the brilliant light of an ideal state. They shim-
> mer, providing an image on that vibrant field upon which the
> trajectory of an individual's life becomes the projected hope of
> others who watch. . . . An admiring public believes that the hu-
> man weakness, cupidity, and hypocrisy in which they are mired
> can actually be overcome. The person who overcomes these vices
> becomes more than a person, he (or sometimes she, albeit rarely
> in the Islamic past) becomes semi-transparent; such a person's
> actions and words reveal the illumination from a source that
> would remain hidden if not for the reflective screen that their
> burnished hearts provide.

Is it any wonder Sheikh Hamza's favorite public version of himself is this one? And what to make of the responsibilities saints assume with respect to those who see them as exemplary and as their
access to the sacred mysteries and the sacred law?

Omar Nawaz once suggested to me that the burden of leadership that leaders like Imam Zaid and Sheikh Hamza take on is so significant and so grave that Muslims should do everything within their power to avoid it. The Muslim who leads no one is responsible for no one's soul but his own when facing Allah on the Day of Judgment; the Muslim who takes the souls of others under his protection has to answer for every single one of his followers. Presented with this idea, Hamza replied: "Exactly."

FIVE

631 Jackson Street

Her life's work done, she is now gone.

—Zaid Shakir

Zaytuna moved to Berkeley and turned into a college, so there was no use for the land.

—Sayyid Hesham al-Alusi

The nostalgia that hangs around Zaytuna and preoccupies so many of the Muslims who consider themselves Zaytunies does not seek home only in the days of the Prophet and his companions, nor some late-medieval Moroccan saint, nor even the precolonial Islamic scholarship that for centuries shaped the rule of law in the Muslim world. Many of the Muslims who support the college and remain a part of the broader community are homesick for their own early days on a campus just off California State Route 92 in Hayward, the trademarked "Heart of the Bay," about twenty miles south of Berkeley. Some of the Zaytunies are still sick over a fallen tree.

As Sheikh Hamza remembers it, the idea for Zaytuna College took root back as long ago as 2000, when he met with the Catholic nun Marianne Farina, a professor at the Graduate Theological Union's Dominican School of Philosophy and Theology, under the wooden beams of the yurt on the institute's property in Hayward. Fabric hung all around. Dr. Hatem was there, as well. And when Hamza tells of that meeting, as he did during Zaytuna's convocation, it takes on the quality of a creation story: "The seed was planted by Sister Marianne Farina many, many years ago." In the beginning there was the yurt. In the beginning there was 631 Jackson Street. The place itself was a revelation.

In essence, what Sister Farina said in that big round tent that seems to have affected Hamza so deeply was this: "*You're one-fourth of the world's population. Where are the Muslim colleges? Where's the Muslim seminary to teach Muslims? You need to do it.* Zaytuna should think about that." For Sheikh Hamza, this marks what he calls the "turning point." For four years Zaytuna Institute had been attracting people to Hayward for classes and fellowship, something it would continue to do for nearly another decade. But they could do more. It would begin with a seminary, of course, which would take another four years and the help of Imam Zaid and Zaytuna scholars Yahya Rhodus and Ali Amer to organize.

The original two-acre Hayward campus was a sort of haven for the early Zaytunies, who would descend on the site from all over the Bay Area. Prior to Zaytuna's taking over, the plot had been abandoned; the area's homeless had often taken up residence.

Immediately off the highway, when students and visitors passed through the gates they came upon the main hall, known within the community as the madrasah. The hall was divided inside by a decorative mahogany screen separating the brothers from the sisters. Both sides had a view of the scholar seated on a stage at the front of the room. Just beyond the limits of the campus's lawns stood concrete pillars supporting the BART line running between Richmond and Fremont. When photographer Lonny Shavelson and Oakland writer Fred Setterberg visited Zaytuna for their 2007 book *Under the Dragon: California's New Culture,* they took note that "thousands of commuters sped by each day over tracks skirting the mosque, never dreaming it was there." Their photo essay highlighted the lives of Latino Muslims who had found a religious home at Zaytuna, former Catholics "who switched from English and Arabic to their native Spanish." (Like many of these Muslims, Sheikh Hamza's wife was also of Mexican descent.) There was a vegetable garden. And along one path running toward the back of the property, Sheikh Hamza encouraged students to pick weeds and involve themselves generally in the upkeep of the grounds, suggesting to them that their actions be intentional prayers to Allah "to remove a weed from all of our hearts."

The buildings had Spanish-style roofs, stucco walls, and wooden latticework archways. Shoe racks stood at the door. Loudspeakers would call the community to prayer. And brothers and sisters would make their way along wide covered walkways draped with vines and flowering plants.

One tree at Zaytuna had particular significance; known as the Bowing Tree, this "aging pine," as Imam Zaid would say in a 2005 blog post, was "seemingly bowed by the travails of time into a reverent prayer position." The tree was referred to as "she" and had an "invigorating aroma." She was a graceful mother to "a legion of youthful climbers, her tempting branches all the more accessible" because she bent down. "Some of the greatest contemporary scholars of Islam have sat beneath her shade," wrote Zaid. "Sacred knowledge has been conveyed under her vigilant watch. And from the safety of the refuge she represented, many have paused to watch as winter rain gently caressed the green grass unfolding before her."

Children played in the lawns and gathered in the yurt to memorize the Koran. In 2001, during a near-monthlong summer retreat known as Rihla, organized by the Deen Intensive Foundation, the same yurt was used by the men as sleeping quarters. (*Rihla*, in Arabic, suggests a journey; *deen* means "religion" or "way of life.")

Often drawn initially to Zaytuna Institute by the reputation of Sheikh Hamza and the weekly and biweekly classes he helped organize—taught by a whole array of scholars over the years—the community itself and the fellowship became for many a reason to come back. New Muslims were brought into the community with the declaration known as the *shahada*, said before the community: "There is no god but God, and Muhammad is the messenger of God."

Though for some time her life as a nun took Sister Farina to work as an administrator at St. Mary's College in Indiana, over the years she's been intermittently involved with shaping the scholarly Islamic community in Berkeley. She played a vital role both early and late in establishing the Center for Islamic Studies at the Graduate Theological Union. In fact, it was the school's early commitment to Islam—

pre-9/11, before a Center for Islamic Studies became a university must-have—that brought her to meet with Hamza in the first place. In 2000, shortly after John Donahue arrived at the GTU to serve as president, Sister Farina and her colleague Professor Giv Nassiri, from the Pacific School of Religion, approached him with the idea of surveying the Muslim communities throughout the Bay Area to ask them a few questions: "If a Center for Islamic Studies was to open at the GTU, what would it look like? What would you hope it would look like? And what needs could be met by opening such a center?" Her visit to the yurt in Hayward was part of this broad survey.

"There just isn't enough," she said. And although she was mainly talking about her own institution's hopes for establishing a productive Center for Islamic Studies, one that served certain needs of the local Muslim community as much as it might produce leading Muslim scholars, she seemed to be hinting that Zaytuna likewise had a role to play nationally in establishing a solid foundation for Islamic learning. What she meant was that while there are plenty of Catholic liberal arts colleges, and any number of Jewish liberal arts colleges, there simply wasn't, at the time, a Muslim liberal arts college anywhere in the country. Living for some time among Muslims in Dhaka, Bangladesh, Sister Farina helped to run a liberal arts college that was, as she told me, "full of Muslims." And as early as 2000, she asked Hamza: "Where is it here in the United States?"

And for the record, she's humble—totally dismissive, even—about whatever role she played in the founding of Zaytuna College. "Sheikh Hamza was too generous in his remarks," she once wrote. "It was a simple visit and I was suggesting the need of a Muslim presence at the GTU—not just an occasional class but a 'voice.'"

It seems Sheikh Hamza never said as much to Sister Farina; but if her visit truly was a turning point in his thinking about Zaytuna, what he seems to have recognized during their discussion were the limits she saw, along with her colleagues at the GTU, in an approach to Muslim education that was, in any way, haphazard. Her fact-finding visit to Zaytuna Institute was a signal that at the Graduate Theological Union, it simply would not do any longer to have the occasional class led by Dr. Hatem or Giv Nassiri, who were both hired privately with money raised, apparently within a single extended family, by Ameena Jandali, the cofounder of San Francisco's Islamic Networks Group, and her uncle, Dr. Khalid Siddiqi.

For its part, Zaytuna has existed this way—joyfully, even blessedly, but haphazardly all the same—since its founding in 1996. When Hamza Yusuf returned to California after years of traditional study overseas—in the United Arab Emirates, Saudi Arabia, and North and West Africa—he first completed degrees in religious studies at San Jose State University and in nursing at Imperial Valley College. And following that, Sheikh Hamza had been successful organizing classes in Hayward, bringing in scholars to teach them, and offering Arabic to eager converts and lifelong Muslims alike. But, he did not want to have Zaytuna remain just an "advanced religious-studies group," Sister Farina told me. He saw in Zaytuna the "potential for not only training religious leaders, but also training minds, training persons"— in terms of academics as well as religious studies. As with any other religious institutions that run liberal arts colleges, Farina concluded, "Faith is taken seriously but faith isn't the only thing. . . . Faith is taken seriously as part of the whole mix of how we understand our world, and how we look at it." A nun and sheikh met, that seed was planted, and slowly but surely, things would begin to change.

Today, Farina believes it is best that Zaytuna remained a Muslim project, one that grew out of the community and tries, as much as possible, to remain in touch with Muslims throughout the Bay area. Depending on who you ask, they are more or less successful at this. So Zaytuna students attended *jummah* prayers with the Muslim Students Association at UC Berkeley. Imam Zaid continues to offer classes and weekly sermons at Oakland's storefront Lighthouse Mosque, which he founded in 2007 and then gave over to Imam Abdul Latif Finch and Amir Sundiata Al-Rashid. Usama Canon's Ta'leef Collective, which took over the Zaytuna Institute outreach program and continues to reach converts throughout the Bay, goes a long way to bring together the scholarship of the college with the spiritual and cultural practices of young Muslims. And to the extent that the connections between the GTU and Zaytuna and organizations like the Islamic Networks Group and Ta'leef Collective remain strong, Farina's hopes for the Center for Islamic Studies, run today by Muslim scholar Munir Jiwa, are more or less the same. "Our communities," she said, "are giving shape to what we're becoming." And unlike other Islamic studies departments in the country (she cited Georgetown), "Zaytuna is born out of the people legitimately and authentically saying what their needs are." Now, what must shape the college's ongoing scholarly commitment to both the *ummah* and non-Muslim communities like the GTU (offering what Farina called "moral support") is a continuing recognition from Zaytuna "that in meeting those needs local communities have to be involved."

When I asked some of the students what they thought about the relationship of Zaytuna to their community at large, and what circumstances the three founders might have been responding to in the Bay Area and across the country when they decided to open the college, Faatimah Knight, the Brooklyn native, seemed almost confused by the question. In her mind and certainly with all due respect, that the school had founders at all seemed beside the point. Even in this new, specifically Western, specifically academic incarnation, to her Zaytuna College seemed "organic." Even from her place within the admittedly small and somewhat cloistered early days of the institution, she said it had always felt that Zaytuna was a product of the community, that it "comes directly from" them and the growing number of people who participate in it. By her account, Zaytuna is a "natural institution"; that it exists now as an American college is not because Sheikh Hamza, or Imam Zaid, or Dr. Hatem wanted it to exist, but rather because the "people wanted it."

Beginning as early as the *iftar* meal that followed the convocation, students told me of complete strangers approaching them to say how proud they were of them. What often came next was a request that the students not hesitate to ask, Faatimah reported, "if you need anything." And though these specific ideas were much discussed in my conversations about the school—that Zaytuna reflected a growing desire in the community for a Muslim school of higher learning, that it was an institution for the people and by the people—it wasn't until I asked the students directly, suggesting their unusual situation relative to the funds raised (and in some cases, food donated) on their specific behalf, that I could see what enormous pressure they were under as a result.

When I first raised the possibility, the older Zaytunie, Rasheeda, said she'd never thought about it quite like that. And yet, she was, after a few moments, able to articulate her situation better than the rest, and it may be that whatever additional pressures were involved in belonging to this first class of the nation's first Muslim college required no actual thinking at all. Given the chance to enroll, her being there suddenly became a religious imperative. "There was something I feel that I have to give back anyway." That's what it means to be a Muslim. And that, she said, was "why I wanted to come to Zaytuna." Before the year began, she may have known abstractly that there would be this "additional level of consideration," as she put it—the community's eyes would be on her, these specific and beloved scholars would correct her work—and that she, like the rest of the Zaytunies, had something to prove. But, by her coming here and seeing the support in action—knowing that American Muslims she might never meet were by and large responsible for the lights coming on and the water running, the scholars teaching and the administrators running the show behind the scenes—everything became real. It didn't take long, she said, before "I had to think about what I was doing with what they were giving me." Indeed, no one wanted to waste the support being extended by Muslims around the country.

From the founders' point of view, central to succeeding in this will mean becoming an accredited institution. This would seem to matter less to those students in the first class who already have undergraduate degrees—Chris, say, or Adnan, Jamye, Hadeel, Dustin, or Rasheeda. For that matter, with neither a guarantee nor really much hope that an accreditation review will go through by the time this class graduates, even the true freshmen—Leenah, Mahassin, Haroon, and Faatimah—can't possibly care all that much. See, as much as the school must, with the long view, strive to meet standards laid out by the Western Association of Schools and Colleges—sustainability beyond the lives of the founders, a general education curriculum, and policies establishing academic freedom and nondiscrimination, to name only a few—those details mean nothing compared with the fact that, in Faatimah's words: "Wow, I found an institution that matched who I am."

On this point, though, it might also be said that standards of accreditation are designed to be more or less invisible, integrated seamlessly into the daily life and future plans of any school. Of course, it might likewise be said that who Faatimah is—and who any of these students are—has as much to do with a belief in academic freedom, intellectual integrity and accountability, and nondiscrimination, as it does with their submission to Islam and belief that there is no god but God. Most likely, there may simply be no telling where one sort of belief ends and the other begins, or really whether they're different beliefs at all.

Is Zaytuna a place that matches who you are? I asked a group of students. Is it like you?

Sumaya said simply, "Yes."

Rasheeda went a little further: "Zaytuna is like what I want to be."

But for these students, it wasn't always so easy to remember that before they were here, Zaytuna had been like what a whole lot of Muslims wanted to be.

One of these was a white convert named Zachary Twist, a long-time member of the community who served for a time as director of operations and programs at Zaytuna Institute. Zachary, who introduced himself to me as "Zakariyya," was a student and admirer of Sheikh Hamza. Over time, Hamza and the early Zaytuna community more generally had come to rely on Zachary's skills in organizing and development. In all the time I spent with him—first at the Lighthouse Mosque, then post-*jummah* lunches in Berkeley, and various fund-raisers and lectures and celebrations throughout the Bay—Zachary never had anything bad to say about anyone and nothing but encouraging words for the college, its scholars, and the students, which seemed in keeping with Koranic prohibitions against gossip and backbiting. Still, there was something particular about his nostalgia for the old Zaytuna that gave me the impression that he felt left behind in the move from Hayward to Berkeley. Perhaps it was the way he talked about others who felt left behind.

By Zachary's account, during the early days of the institute, the whole operation was the brainchild of Sheikh Hamza, who might also occasionally use Zaytuna to indulge a whim. The focus of the community began with Sheikh Hamza's focus, and this continued for years.

When, for instance, Sheikh Hamza wanted a certain class offered on the campus, said Zachary, that class would start right up. Members of the community assumed whatever tasks they were qualified for—groundskeeping, gardening, teaching, organizing, editing, fund raising, cooking—because Hamza wanted things done and they served the community he was building. The result was energizing.

Likewise, when Hamza wanted to create *Seasons*, a semiannual publication of writings on classical Islam, Muslim scholarship, poetry, and other matters relevant to the community, the journal simply got made. He was editor in chief and directed a host of other editors. A disclaimer at the bottom of the table of contents noted: "We support the articles in this journal in that they reflect intelligent discourse in our community whether or not they reflect the philosophy of Zaytuna Institute." Although one scholar whose articles you could be sure reflected the philosophy of Zaytuna Institute was Sheikh Hamza. What he might say in his lectures over the years would find some permanence in his journal.

And *Seasons* was as much a place for devotion as it was for the finer points of Arabic linguistics or the shariah, an approach to scholarship that he brought with him to the founding of a liberal arts college. Concluding a 2005 essay on Islamic "tolerance," which he rooted in a comprehensive study of "the semantic field the word [*sam ha*] reveals," Sheikh Hamza noted: "Islam is much maligned these days, and it is incumbent on those who have even a sense of its sublime nature and heavenly character to defend it by living it, to spread it by embodying it, and to pass it on by preserving it."

September 11 had marked a turning point, of course, since with the attacks Sheikh Hamza's stature had risen; he'd become a national figure, a spokesperson for the community. An adviser to the president. (Or, again, "Bush's pet Muslim.") With his responsibilities stretching far beyond Hayward, all this meant that he would have less time actually with the community. And yet, by word of mouth and as Sheikh Hamza continued to distribute his lectures and sermons on audiotape and CD, Zaytuna Institute began to develop a reputation around the country—and increasingly throughout the world—for the way it transmitted sacred knowledge and offered non-Muslims a look at the *ummah*.

In 2003, as his own responsibilities were becoming too much, Hamza invited Imam Zaid, a convert like himself, to join the scholars at Zaytuna. Zaid had developed a reputation for his scholarship and passion as the founder of Masjid Al-Islam in New Haven, Connecticut; like Sheikh Hamza, he had spent years in the Middle East studying Islam. Getting the call, Zaid chose to pack up, leaving the New Haven mosque and its three hundred congregants in the hands of Imam Dawood Yasin, and moved West. Originally from Berkeley, California, Zaid's move to Zaytuna represented a kind of homecoming.

With Imam Zaid's arrival as a scholar-in-residence, the institute was reinvigorated once again, despite Hamza's more regular absences. By Zachary's account, the community only increased its appeal and activities. There were classes seven days a week, classes in the evenings, weekend classes all day. All weekend the commons were filled with families. And suddenly Imam Zaid was at the center; his enthusiasm seemed boundless. He wanted to respond to all the needs of the community, teaching class after class after class, whether in the Koran, Arabic, or finer points of law. Zaid also took on the development of the seminary program and, with Dr. Hatem in the background, pushed hard for the development of the college.

Thinking this way about the future of Zaytuna became possible largely because, as the scholars' appeal grew as national and international Muslim leaders—both Sheikh Hamza and to a lesser extent Imam Zaid—their speaking engagements and other appearances began to be a great revenue source for the institute. And while Hamza and Zaid raised funds nationally toward what they both saw as a historic effort of the seminary and the college, which could ultimately train many fewer, full-time students, the community itself became a drain on those resources.

Because while the prominence and visibility of Zaytuna Institute in Hayward increased—through an online presence and those lectures on CD, cassette tapes, and DVDs; by publishing *Seasons* and sending its scholars around the country and the world—from a distance the institute seemed to offer something more than what it ever could be. To some, it looked completely self-sustaining. Zachary told me about people who would arrive in Hayward, luggage in hand, just waiting to move in at the Zaytuna campus. Zachary told me of families who had given up another life elsewhere in the country because they'd seen Hamza or Zaid in their hometown or they'd viewed clips of their sermons and speeches on the Internet. And yet, in truth, Zaytuna was not set up for that. And as much as those behind the institute might have liked to fold social services and permanent housing into its religious educational mission, it simply wasn't possible then. For the first time ever, perhaps, Zaytunies grew disgruntled. Some then moved away.

Zachary also told me that all the while the community continued to grow—even as a few families left or decided not to make the trip to Hayward on the weekends—he also found himself having occasionally to make trips to campus in the middle of the night to ward off would-be intruders, vandals, and thieves. A few break-ins led to a general feeling of insecurity. He told me the problem was within the community. Muslim thieves.

At a certain point, Zachary concluded, the center simply wasn't holding. With Hamza pulled in any number of directions and Imam Zaid intensely focused on the pilot seminary program that would eventually graduate Ebad, it became difficult for anyone to manage the increasing, and increasingly petty, concerns of the community. Even the property itself began to feel like a drain. Its upkeep was expensive and the Muslims of Hayward and the rest of the Bay Area weren't providing anything like the financial support Hamza and Zaid had been able to raise around the country.

Syed Mubeen Saifullah, the secretary of Zaytuna's board of trustees, has reported that as the pilot seminary program came to a successful close, and as the scholars continued to debate over what would come next, it became increasingly clear that only about 10 percent of the money raised for the future of Zaytuna was coming from the community itself. "That was a wake-up call to do something much bigger and more inspiring," Saifullah has said. "This is why Zaytuna exists," he continued to reporter Sameea Kamal, writing in the Muslim-interest magazine *Illume.* "We need the next generation of scholars and thinkers in our community and we need to do it in a place where there's access to the best amount of resources in the country." And in the Bay, that's in Berkeley. Hayward wouldn't work. "So we decided to move."

Though she had often been seen by the Zaytunies as a model of humility, bending forward before God, Zaytuna's Bowing Tree could not bow forever. It was predicted in the Koran that her time would come: "The stars and the trees prostrate [unto Him]." One night she fell; she could only bend so much. Imam Zaid wrote her eulogy in 2005, and the tree became the image of a fallen Muslim. "It should have come as no surprise when on a fateful, rainy winter night, she completed her devotion, prostrating totally to her Lord. Her majestic head nestled firmly upon the ground, her massive trunk oriented towards the prayer direction, her toes, partially uprooted, curved beneath her. Her life's work done, she is now gone."

Zaid's reflection concluded with a note about human mortality and the breathtaking fact of our own impermanence, a fact that resides at the heart of both the nostalgia and the humility of the Muslims Imam Zaid is trying to inspire. "There is no permanence in this lower abode. Perhaps it is not coincidental that the very Koranic chapter that mentions the prostration of trees also reminds us, *All on earth will perish.*"

After years of use, the hall they gathered in had been dedicated May 13, 2003—the twelfth day of Rabi'a al-Awwal, 1424, in the Islamic calendar, the birthday of the Prophet—and named for Sayyid Hesham al-Alusi, a philanthropist and cofounder of Zaytuna Institute. Al-Alusi was an Iraqi-born engineer who worked toward his PhD at UC Berkeley in the late 1960s, returned to Iraq in 1970 to teach at the University of Baghdad, and then resettled for good in the Bay Area in 1980.

And yet, by at least one account, al-Alusi wasn't completely pleased with the decisions being made behind the scenes to limit the scope and the level of outreach in order to form the college. And he wasn't alone. Near the end, Zachary Twist had found himself less and less central to the decision-making at Zaytuna. And though he told me the story first in a way that suggests it was simply time for him to move on and do something else for the Bay Area Muslim community—which he's certainly done, while maintaining ties to Zaytuna—in a second telling it was clear to me that he was somewhat disappointed in the direction Zaytuna was taking, to say nothing about the fact that over the years he was, in effect, replaced by newcomers.

So it should have come as no surprise. In July 2007, Zaytuna's leaders gathered the community for a meeting in the institute's madrasah, al-Alusi Hall. It was all over. Zaytuna Institute would end. Zaytuna College would be the future. The gears had already begun moving and there was no stopping them. At one point during the meeting, the crowd grew so upset—tearful, angry—that Sheikh Hamza simply walked out.

Near the door hung the plaque designed for the dedication of the hall for al-Alusi; Hamza had written an untitled poem in honor of the day and the man. And, of course, Allah. The original is in Arabic. The English translation reads:

As minutes and seconds pass by
and time takes its toll on a place
An age brings an end to all things
built upon stones without grace

When Zaytuna left Hayward, Hesham al-Alusi has said, "Things fell apart." Asked about this by the *Illumine* reporter Kamal, Dr. Hatem put it a little differently: "After Zaytuna relocated to Berkeley, the property's maintenance was transitioned to the community. Unfortunately the proper maintenance of the property proved to be

a time-consuming effort which wasn't scalable by the community."
This is quintessential Hatem.

The property is still owned by the college but it's hardly used
at all anymore. A prison convert and old-time Zaytunie named An-
sary told me about an eccentric friend with a knack for construction
work who had parked his RV on the property and was scraping by.
Though selling the property proved difficult during the economic
downturn that coincided with the transition from Hayward to Berkeley, everyone hopes that 631 Jackson Street will remain the address
of Muslims.

Despite whatever hard feelings remain among some Zaytunies
who were left behind in and around Hayward, you don't sense there
are really that many regrets—even in Zachary Twist, who now chairs
the board of directors of an Islamic elementary school in Union City,
California, called Northstar, and who retains strong ties to the scholars and students at Zaytuna College. And through all the nostalgia,
you likewise get no sense of regret from the founders of Zaytuna
College. Moving the often unwieldy campus in Hayward to the basement classrooms of an underused Baptist seminary became the best
of all possible moves for Sheikh Hamza, Imam Zaid, and Dr. Hatem.

Like the tree that symbolized the humility of Islam and, in its
way, the dangers of grasping beyond one's reach, the life's work of
Zaytuna Institute, 631 Jackson Street, Hayward, is done. She is now
gone. There's another tree now that lights the way—*zaytunah*, of
course, is the olive's oil that produces light without fire.

SIX

The Dear Self

Ricky, the second one, is nervous, high-strung, and talented. For a boy of almost seventeen, he stays much too
close to home. In a way this is good; in a way it is not. He
should get out more, make friends with some of his peers.
And yet, I was also somewhat a loner as a teenager, I still
am, so what can I say. He'll probably do all right.
                          —Richelene Mitchell, January 30, 1973

If to understand what stands behind the life and work of Sheikh
Hamza Yusuf it seems appropriate to look to the late-medieval saint
Ahmad Zarruq, to do the same for Imam Zaid Shakir it seems most
natural to turn to his mother, whose death of an aneurism at forty-
one, he's written, "catalyzed my desire to know God." But the influence Zaid's mother had on his becoming a Muslim—and more, this
particular Muslim leader—has much less to do with her tragic, early
death, it seems, than with the life she presented him raising seven
kids as a single mother, a "welfare mother," in the housing projects of
Atlanta, Georgia, and New Britain, Connecticut.

Their appeal and influence among Muslims is more complicated
than can be conveyed by a description of their personalities or the
self-styling that has transformed Sheikh Hamza into what the Zaytuna student Dustin Craun one day called "a global head of state"
and Imam Zaid into "the Imam of America." (The way these phrases
rolled off Dustin's tongue left the impression that they were common ways within the community of describing the two men.) And it's
likewise too simple to say that either Imam Zaid or Sheikh Hamza
might be limited in their activities or interests in the classroom, or
the mosque, or a clearing at the top of a hill, by some notion that
either of them has a particular role to fill at Zaytuna, in the nation,
or around the world.

And yet, when Zaid Shakir tells the story about coming into his own Islam, he roots it in a particular American experience. It's a black experience. We'd all heard it on the top of that hill: Shaytan was the first racist. When I first witnessed him in the mosque, Zaid again seemed especially concerned with what it means to be black in America. Paraphrasing Malcolm X, or El-Hajj Malik El-Shabazz, Zaid reminded the congregation of what that black leader had come to see in the traditional Islam he turned to near the end of his life: "Islam has done much to address the race problem in the Muslim world. . . . Perhaps if Americans could study and understand Islam it could help to address the race problem in America." And though in the same sermon he would emphasize the diversity of the group— "there are people representing thirty or forty different ethnicities and national origins, brought together by Allah"—there was also the sense that in invoking Malcolm X, he was preaching to the choir: "And many of you remember that quote. This is something we have to work towards."

Imam Zaid's experience of the race problem in America stretches back as far as he can remember, back to when his name was Ricky Mitchell and he lived in the care of his mother, Richelene. In his autobiographical essay "The Making of a Muslim," which begins his 2005 book *Scattered Pictures*, published by Zaytuna Institute, Zaid calls to mind a childhood "couched in black." Though born in Berkeley in 1956, his earliest memories come from the Carver Homes of Southwest Atlanta, a housing project where his mother had resettled to be close to family after separating from Zaid's father, a former Navy man turned jazz musician. (His father's career in music, Zaid says, had "led to instability in the family." Richelene remembered him as an "evil, evil man!") At the Carver Homes and in his elementary school and even on trips to his family's farm in tiny Hamilton, Georgia, where he remembers going out to pick cotton, it was clear that the world young Ricky belonged to was a black one. It was the world of his mother.

When the family moved to New Britain to reunite—albeit only briefly—with his father, who had landed a steady job at a local Sears store, they again found themselves in a housing project, although when they moved into Pinnacle Heights, the community was still mainly white. This would change entirely over the next decade of white flight, Zaid writes in "The Making of a Muslim," as "the Irish 'Smiths' were replaced with the African American 'Johnsons.'" And so on: "The Italian 'Mirantes' two doors down were to be replaced by the African American 'Daniels.' On the other side of our unit, the Jewish 'Prices' were to be replaced by another African American family." The white families still living in Pinnacle Heights in the year Ricky started high school, he says, were simply "families too poor to move elsewhere."

Over the years the family grew to include seven children, one older sister and five younger siblings. When Richelene finally left their domineering father, after he'd made threats against her and the kids, she assumed complete responsibility for raising them. So far away from her family in the South, the burden was hers alone. Zaid's own memories of these times bring together the struggles of a welfare mother with the relentlessness of her activist and intellectual life. She wrote lots of letters to the local papers. Zaid proudly remembers, "She was an active reader and a controversial writer. Her editorials and articles regularly appeared in the *New Britain Herald* and the *Hartford Courant.* Her poignant views on issues relating to race and social justice earned her the wrath of various white supremacy groups who would frequently send threatening hate mail to our home."

Ricky read some of those letters, and years later, he writes, "they would help fuel my anti-Americanism." But white supremacy wasn't only the province of strangers at a distance. A strong athlete growing up, Ricky had a football coach who would drive by to gather his players from the projects every morning for practice while the season was on; once the season was over, though, Ricky and those other black kids were invisible to him. He got not even a glance in the school's hallways. Zaid remembers it in language that sounds a lot like his letter-writing mother: "This callous exploitation was not lost on me."

And yet, while Zaid's public statements, even about himself, often seem modeled on what he calls his mother's "deep literary yearning," and her "keen intellect, and poetic sensitivity," her own public expression is just a fraction of what shaped her son's view of social justice and why her life helped make him the Muslim he became. Richelene Mitchell kept a diary for the year 1973. And very much of it sounds like this, from October 27. "Dear Self," she wrote:

> I'm sick, sick, and sick of this dreary dead-end existence I'm sick, sick, sick of being stuck here in this junk-filled house with no outlet, no money, no nothing. Sewing machine out of order; TV out of order; refrigerator out of order; stove just making it; winter coming up with its necessities; and no money in sight to repair, replace, or buy anything! I'm sick to my soul of scraping, squeezing, and scrounging.

This is the world Zaid Shakir knew as a young man. And in 2007, now through his own imprint New Islamic Directions, as an imam he would publish his mother's diary from 1973, *Dear Self: A Year in the Life of a Welfare Mother*. The year was filled with entries that are alternately, as he notes, "lively and lengthy" and "cold, short, and blunt." The whole thing couched in black.

And as December approached its end that year, she looked back, accounting for just a few "small drippings of joy" alongside the "tears and gall" that characterized her days. Her writing amounts to hundreds of pages and ultimately ends in darkness, with thirteen days left in 1973. "Sometimes during my reflections with you, self," she wrote, "I think I offered the theory that the drippings of joy we get are sweet enough to overpower the gall. But they aren't. The drippings are saccharine, a little sweet, but bitter to the aftertaste. The bitterness prevails." That a reader of his mother's diary might walk away knowing this fact about the lives of the "underclass," as he calls it, is in the end all Zaid can hope for in offering her reflections to the world. "I am absolutely confident," he notes in the book's introduction, "that no one will read our mother's words without a greatly enhanced understanding of the lives and struggles of the urban poor. If this is indeed the case, she did not pen these words in vain, and a new reality for

poor folks in America has shined its dawning rays on a better world."
His life's work as an imam and as a scholar has been to make good on
this promise of his mother's diary. His most basic charge to American
Muslims—who are, he has written, "by and large a privileged class in
this country"—is that they might "conceive of the lives lived by the
poor." To start, he's offered the American *ummah* his own life. And
the *ummah* loves him.

Beyond revealing a life lived by one poor woman, Richelene Mitchell's diary also offers a mother's perspective on the son she most often
worried about. Comparing her own children to talented boys down
the street, Richelene noted at the end of February 1973:

> Perhaps one of us, as insignificant as we can think we are, can be
> a leader. . . . We may well have the makings of leaders in our
> midst—in Orlick and Kendrick. They are extremely intelligent
> twin boys who live on this block, with their divorced mother. . . .
> I see no signals of leadership in my own, so far. But if they grow
> up to be decent, stable, supportive citizens, I'll have no quarrels
> with life. One thing I believe, leaders are born not made. . . . So
> I'll not aggravate myself and my children by trying to mold them
> into something they are not.

Her son Ricky was no leader back then. No, he was "poor Ricky,"
the boy home nursing the feet and ankle he'd injured playing sports.
The boy who stayed too close to home for someone seventeen years
old. The boy who was "so tall, so good-looking, so bright, so talented,
so basically good-natured, but so emotional, so high-strung, so tem-
peramental, so sensitive, so suggestible, so much alone." Having seen
the world change somewhat—America in 1973 was "being forced,"
she said, "into more acceptance of black men at all levels"—she hoped
he might excel in art, since he'd recently admitted, after some apparent struggles, that he was going nowhere with high school math. And
despite Richelene's own misgivings about athletics as a "black man's
best hope of shining in life," she felt truly sorry for Ricky as he faced

the disappointment of what she called his "ill-starred feet." Both lon-
ers, she saw much of herself in her son, and you get the sense that
when she hoped and prayed to her "dear self" that he might someday find something he could be excellent at, that he might "make it
through without too much inner turmoil," you get the sense she's
hoping and praying for Richelene as much as for poor Ricky.

At the end of January, she wrote, "He'll probably do all right."
And she wasn't wrong. Ricky would do all right. Though looking
back, you might say it's largely because Richelene never really did.

In March 1975, having struggled openly with both depression and
epilepsy, Richelene Mitchell died after an aneurism ruined her brain
and she fell into a coma lasting several days. Her death, as he's said,
propelled Ricky out into the world, though somewhat haplessly at
first. That summer he left part-time jobs in Connecticut and traveled
to Washington, DC, as a young political activist with communist ambitions. He went to Atlanta to see family. Returning North, the next
semester he left Central Connecticut State College, where he'd en-
rolled in the fall of 1974—"there was no effort made to talk me out of
leaving"—and lived briefly with his father in Michigan before returning to Connecticut once again, now with fewer prospects than ever.
The "old apartment" his mother called home was overflowing; Zaid's
oldest sister, now a mother of three, had taken over the place in New
Britain with her husband, and they'd made room for the two youngest Mitchells, as well. This left no room for Ricky.

Zaid's enlistment that year in the Air Force was the direct result,
he often says, of the "poverty draft," an influence he sees at work over
the past decade, as well, as the United States filled the branches of its
military to fight wars in Iraq and Afghanistan. And so, when he dis-
cusses his own recruitment into the armed forces, in the same breath
he'll usually offer a sharp critique of the military industrial complex
and call the whole situation at the time "really depressing," especially given the leftist political leanings he'd taken from his mother
and then worked to develop at the state college. First there was basic
training in San Antonio, then technical school in Denver, and finally

a permanent posting at Barksdale Air Force Base outside Shreveport, Louisiana. Through it all the fact remained, depressing as it was, that Uncle Sam would put food on a plate and make sure he had a place to sleep.

With the complete unmooring that accompanied the death of his mother, for Zaid the mid-1970s was marked by restlessness and tension in his religious life. Convinced during those few early months in college of the "imperialist agenda" behind the Christianity he was raised with though never knew very well, he declared himself an atheist. This went along well with his communism. But for only a very short time.

The way he tells it in "The Making of a Muslim," rediscovering God "happened suddenly and strangely"; it involved his coming upon "one of those small rectangular Christian comic books," tracts that had been popularized in the early '70s by the evangelical Jack Chick. This particular comic made the case not for Christianity specifically, but rather for something more basic: "His argument," Zaid remembers, "was basically the argument of causation, that it was impossible to create something from nothing, no matter how hard intelligent minds tried." The tract also argued that nonliving, inorganic substances required a life-giver to grant them "the ability to grow and reproduce." Remember how Yahweh breathed life into the clay. Finally, Zaid was convinced of the notion often called intelligent design, which supposes that our "primal substance" evolved not accidentally—though this isn't exactly what Darwinism says either—but rather by way of a guiding hand from God. Ineloquent and even puerile as it sounds, the comic presented young Ricky Mitchell with a God who was a creator, a life-giver, and an evolver. Chick would say Jesus. Zaid would come to say Allah. "I would later learn that these were all"—creator, life-giver, evolver—"understood as names or attributes of God in Islamic theology."

It's worth noting the irony here that "Chick tracts," as they are known, would come to include bizarre storylines detailing the conversion of Muslim caricatures to Chick's brand of Christianity. The 1994 tract "Allah Had No Son," a title that plays on the Muslim belief that Jesus, though a prophet, was not the son of God, actually opens with a Christian man and his son stumbling upon an imposing mosque where they find a large group of Muslims in *sujud*, bowing over, their foreheads to the ground. The son asks, "What are they doing, daddy?" His father answers, "They're praying to their moon god, son." This, of course, gets the dander up of a burly Muslim, who announces not only that the Koran would condone his killing the man for saying such a thing but also that they expect "a Muslim flag to fly over the White House in the near future." Which means, of course, that "it will be the *end* of Christianity in America."

It's confusing, though. In the comic, everyone's speaking English, but they seem to be in the Middle East. There are camels, and the Muslim in question is dressed in the long, loose-fitting garment called a *thobe*; on his head he wears a kaffiyeh held in place by the cord called an *agal*. Over the course of the comic, the burly Muslim becomes convinced that Muhammad was a charlatan who'd co-opted pagan beliefs in an effort to gain support and power in the Arabian Peninsula; he becomes equally convinced in the truth of Christianity and immediately converts. Although conversion itself is never enough in a Chick tract: the Muslim asserts, "I must tell my people about the moon god."

The Christian father's answer to the man he's just converted cuts to the heart of the matter; the entire story is really about the violence always bubbling away just under the surface of every Muslim. "It may cost you your life," says the Christian man, which was the same point made by *Forbes*'s Tunku Varadajaran in the wake of Fort Hood: it's the quintessential Muslim who "elects to vindicate his religion in an act of messianic violence." In the comic, the new Christian convert, still wearing his kaffiyeh, responds as a true believer: "It will be worth it, because I'll be with my loving Father in heaven for all eternity."

No longer an atheist, Zaid became a religious seeker, though he continued to eschew the underdeveloped Christianity of his youth; instead, fresh to the Air Force, he turned to slightly more esoteric systems, including transcendental meditation and an ultimately dissatisfying study of Eastern mysticism. He also tested the "mucusless diet," he often says, a "healing system" created in the 1920s by the German health advocate and writer Arnold Ehret. The diet, as Ehret wrote, "consists of all kinds of raw and cooked fruits, starchless vegetables, and cooked or raw, mostly green-leaf vegetables," and, when combined with "long or short fasts [and] progressively changing menus of *non-Mucus-Forming Foods*," promised to heal what ailed you.

Nowadays, not only is Imam Zaid keen on mentioning his early dabbling in Ehret's system, but you still see its residue in his emphasis on both compulsory and voluntary Islamic fasting and the restrictions the faith places on food, from what's proper to eat in general to getting animals to submit to the slaughter before they're killed. This includes his own preaching during those early days of the college about the relationship between spiritual and physical health. It's not just the hiking and the meditative breathing of fresh air in the name of Allah; these days Zaid often sounds like his fellow Berkeleyites, food journalist Michael Pollan and farm-to-table restaurateur Alice Waters. His religious teachings include: *If a product's ingredients list is more than a line long, don't buy it. Sunny D is being marketed in our schools by criminals. We're killing our food, and it will kill us. In America, let's change things; let's bring life.*

On the other side of Chick comics, Eastern mysticism, transcendental meditation, and the mucusless diet was Islam. Zaid essentially came to the faith through the 1974 book *Islam in Focus*, by the Egyptian writer Hammudah Abdalati, which, he says, answered all his questions about religion—beginning with the big one: "Who is God?" Abdalati writes:

> In the world, then, there must be a Great Force in action to keep everything in order. . . . They call Him God because He is the Creator and the Chief Architect of the world, the Originator of life and the Provider of all things in existence. He is not a man because no man can create or make another man. He is not an animal, nor is He a plant. He is neither an idol nor is He a statue of any kind because none of these things can make itself or create

anything else. He is not a machine. He is neither the sun nor is He the moon.

Widely used since its publication to perform *dawah*, or invite new Muslims into the *ummah*, *Islam in Focus* was a gift Zaid received from a close friend. And it wasn't long after reading the book that Zaid found himself making the formal declaration of faith at a mosque affiliated with the Imam Warith Deen Mohammed, who within a year of taking the reins in 1975, had disbanded the Nation of Islam, which his father, Elijah Muhammad, had run for more than forty years.

In the spring of 1977, Ricky Mitchell said, "There is no god but God, and Muhammad is his Prophet," and the Muslim was made.

Married now to a woman named Saliah, whom he'd met—and performed *dawah* with—in the Air Force, Zaid had only begun his education. *Islam in Focus* is itself just a slim volume. And in the twenty-five years between his acceptance of Islam and his arrival on Zaytuna's Hayward campus, much of which he spent abroad studying Arabic and theology, his faith would both take sidetracks and deepen tremendously.

He had a near-miss with the ultraconservative Saudi-based Salafi movement, whose emphasis, he's written, "is on purifying the community through the elimination of blame-worthy innovations (*bid'a*), and instilling firm adherence to what they understand to be the creed of the early generation of Muslims"; a letter admitting him to the Islamic University in Medina arrived too late for him to accept. He'd left the United States and was settling in Egypt, studying Arabic. Having completed a bachelor's degree in international relations at American University and a master's degree in political science at Rutgers University, he would spend that coming year in Cairo instead. Had he ended up in Medina, he wrote, "I would have very likely become an influential caller to the Salafi movement in America, although God knows best." And though over the next several years he would preach about Islamic revolution in the United States and defended for a time "extrasystemic political action"—for example, as Laurie Goodstein has pointed out, the "armed struggle" that led to the rise of the Taliban in Afghanistan—he always remained some-where on the fringes of the Salafi movement. With this sense of re-lief, even Zaid admits the dangerous, extremist temptations that exist for American Salafis; although today he would not want to make too much of it: "While it is certainly true that the overwhelming major-ity of Jihadists are Salafist in their approach to Islam, they are a small minority at odds with the mainstream Salafis."

From Egypt, Zaid returned to Connecticut, where with sights newly set on building institutions for Islam in America, he helped found New Haven's Masjid al-Islam, his home for the next six years. He was the mosque's first imam. And there, with a community of "Arabs, Pakistanis, Malaysians, Africans, and European converts," he led battles against many of the same problems Muslims were tackling in other American cities. From New Haven, Zaid looked to New York's Imam Siraj Wahhaj, a cleric who throughout the 1980s revital-ized his little corner of the world—the dangerous, crack-infested cor-ner of Bedford Avenue and Fulton Street in the Bedford-Stuyvesant neighborhood of Brooklyn—through the efforts of his community at Masjid At-Taqwa, or the Mosque of God-Consciousness. In Brook-lyn, the community took to the street—sometimes using muscle, sometimes getting arrested—and ran overnight patrols to move drug dealers out. New Haven's Muslims would join them, and worked Imam Siraj's model at home: "We had our own mini 'war' against the drug dealers in New Haven," Zaid says, "men and women joining us in the middle of the ghetto in the middle of the night—standing between drug pushers and their customers." Joining the anti-drug movement of the late '80s and early '90s within the largely black-led Muslim communities of America's cities was part of Islam itself, which opposes drugs and alcohol on theological grounds; so says the Prophet: "They ask thee concerning wine and gambling. Say: 'In them is great sin, and some profit, for men; but the sin is greater than the profit.'" Zaid himself has said, "Anything that affects clar-ity of the mind, be it physically such as intoxicants, or emotionally or spiritually such as bitterness and anger, must be avoided." Still, it often seemed more to the point that drugs were destroying the

nation's poorest communities—where Zaid had grown up, where his
mother had died, and where he returned to live once again as an
imam. Through the mosque, he'd oversee volunteer overnight security details for New Haven's housing projects, afterschool programs
for latchkey kids, and plans to keep drugs away from schoolchildren.

Who says leaders are born, not made?

Imam Zaid's deepest Islamic education would come overseas, far
away from the neighborhood. Indeed, it had more or less begun,
somewhat strangely perhaps, during his stint in the Air Force while
stationed with his wife, Saliah, in Turkey. Together they organized
study groups at Incirlik Air Base, where they "gained converts," including one, he claims, who became a Muslim "after placing his face
on the ground during the prayer, which he had joined out of boredom." Although, admittedly, their propagating Islam in Incirlik
seems to have had little to do with their being abroad; in fact, Turkey's official secularism ended up putting the kibosh on Zaid and
Saliah's evening religion classes. A Turkish base commander stepped
in to enforce the law. To Zaid this didn't seem right or fair: "When
we asked him why the laws didn't apply to all the Christians who
were openly organizing and propagating their religion on the base,
he had no answer."

After founding the mosque in New Haven and serving as imam
for more than half a decade, Zaid would again leave the United
States, this time for Syria. Despite measurable growth in New Haven's increasingly devout community, Zaid had come to realize that
he didn't know Islam in the way he believed it could be known. He
didn't possess the sacred knowledge of those whose books he read.
No matter the regular spiritual retreats with the masjid, whole nights
of Ramadan spent in the mosque in devotional prayer, or regular
group study of the Koran and various hadith of the Prophet, Zaid
simply hadn't yet taken seriously Islam's intellectual tradition. He'd
studied, but he had never really studied. He'd lived and led communities as a Muslim, but he hadn't yet achieved what he believed Islam
was ultimately leading him—and everyone—to. He would learn in

Syria that Islam leads the Muslim to abandon ideologies and to dis-
cover his own humanity.

Over nearly seven years, this was the lesson he would learn from
his scholars as they pored over the Koran and the tradition of sayings and reports of the Prophet that surround it. It was the lesson
of the Arabic language and Zaid's studies into Islamic law, where his
fluency in one expanded his fluency in the other. Away from the race
problem he'd always faced in America's neighborhoods, Zaid got his
first real taste in Syria of what he'd later preach about Malcolm X's
move from the ideological black separatism of the Nation of Islam to
his embrace of traditional Islam: "True manhood was not to be found
in an ideology, and I had been approaching Islam as an ideology. . . .
Being in the company of righteous men and women who had worked
consciously and scrupulously for years to refine their true humanity
enabled me to see my own." And so it was that his time in Syria also
convinced him finally of "the narrowness of the Salafi approach to
Islam." Here was the rare miracle of the religious life, where deepening one's knowledge also serves to broaden one's vision.

As he reflects on it, Zaid's time in Syria also worked on him in
two other ways. As life overseas often does, it offered new possibilities and novel reasons to reflect on both his roots and his rootlessness
in America. Arabs are more aware than most of their lineage—the
phrase "the son of" is common in Arabic names—and when faced
with applications to school, Zaid Shakir, "the son of Donald," had
little more to say. "Here the dialogue would end. I did not know my
paternal grandfather's name." So he became Zaid Shakir, *al-Amriki*,
the American, named for the country whose founding and original
sin, he believed, were at some level responsible for the persistent
inequality that continued to ruin the neighborhoods he had always
called home, and that had left his mother, to the end, with her pre-
vailing bitterness and gall.

At the same time, he'd seen Islam at work improving the lives of
the Muslims in Imam Siraj's Brooklyn. He'd done similar good in
New Haven, although he wasn't convinced, looking back at the work
of Masjid al-Islam, that improving the condition of his neighbors was

ever deeply rooted enough in Islamic notions of justice or mercy. He admits that his knowledge of Islam itself simply wasn't deep enough back then. All the while, Zaid's commitments had been somewhat divided. Looking back, his leadership of the New Haven mosque seemed to be yet another expression of the narrow ideologies of the revolutionary and black liberationist movements he'd known in college, or even that of the Salafis he'd sided with, albeit uncomfortably, as a young Muslim. In various ways the poor neighborhoods of New Haven had improved, but, in Zaid's eyes, "that betterment was a residual consequence . . . not a purposeful goal." An American Muslim abroad, he had designs on changing that course when he returned.

The lessons Zaid learned in Syria while he wasn't studying Arabic and the Koran were just as important as those he took from books and scholars. A friend would often take him to visit family in the town of Hama, an all-Muslim city where, in February 1982, a rebellion of Sunni Islamists was brutally suppressed by order of the Syrian regime of Hafez al-Assad. Estimates of those killed, the vast majority civilians, during the twenty-seven-day assault, range between ten thousand and forty thousand. What Zaid found in Hama, even fifteen years later, was a first real taste of what Islamic revolution might look like: "The devastation was not just the physical destruction to be seen in the affected neighborhoods—looted museums, gutted buildings, and the holes and imprints of bullets, tank shells, and artillery rounds—but also in the faces of widows, widowers, and orphans." Before this, revolution had been a way to imagine the course to a better world; he'd preached it at the mosque. He'd written of it in pamphlets. He'd believed in it. Then in Hama he got "to see up close the human cost of real revolution." Detroit and Oakland and New Haven and Bedford-Stuyvesant may look bad, but they didn't look like Hama, which was in some places essentially razed. And strange as it must have seemed at the time, American problems didn't seem quite so unmanageable anymore. In fact, when you remove the blinders many Muslims wear and take a hard look at the Muslim world as a "real human society with real human problems," he's said, "certain aspects of American society start to look really good." Good enough to return to "as we grope along as a society into this new century."

To say that Imam Zaid's return from Syria to New Haven was not all it might have been would be something of an understatement. While he'd been away, the masjid's chemistry had been "shattered by migrations, divisions, and divorces that ravaged the community." Fresh from the devastation still left behind in Hama, American pettiness would send him packing. The place had changed—to be sure, he'd been changed, too—and it was time he moved on. Just eighteen months later he lit out for California to join Sheikh Hamza Yusuf at Zaytuna Institute. The rest, as he says, will be history.

SEVEN

Reviving the Spirit

Nobody knows how a Muslim college in America should
behave. . . . We will always be different, because we should be.
—Omar Nawaz

Needless to say, students must spend at least two hours of
studying for each in-class hour, which means 6–8 hours
(minimum) of outside class study per week is needed for
language learning.
—Ustadh Abdullah bin Hamid Ali,
Intermediate Arabic I syllabus

As with most American colleges, in late December Zaytuna grew
very still. The scholars and students had set off for winter break,
which for many of them included the annual conference in Toronto
called Reviving the Islamic Spirit. The convention was something
to look forward to; thousands of Muslims all in one place, listening
to a whole host of scholars reflect on the state of the *ummah*. The
theme this year was "Rules for the Road of Life: Reviving the Ten
Commandments." For Imam Zaid and Sheikh Hamza, part of the
message would inevitably be the place Zaytuna College could have
in everyone's lives.

While they were all in Toronto, I was in Berkeley, strolling
the halls of Zaytuna one morning hoping to encounter someone—
anyone. I entered through the foyer and passed by the library. It was
dark. There was almost nothing to it. From the corridor that brings
together the classrooms and the administrative offices, I overheard
Omar Nawaz in discussion with someone whose voice I didn't recognize. They seemed to be the only ones around, and their conversation was about future hires. Deciding these were private matters, I

turned around and walked back out the door. At least I knew Omar was around. Later in the day I arranged to join him early the next morning for coffee.

When we sat down together the next day, I learned from Omar that the state of Zaytuna was strong. And he wasn't just saying that, he said. Not surprisingly, everyone was excited to have gotten through the first term; things had gone even better than Omar had expected. Two days before they all left, the faculty, staff, and students had all sort of checked in and discussed how things were going—the students had been exhausted but remained excited. Omar measured this a success, generally.

He had entered the school year believing there would be any number of difficult adjustments for both the scholars and the students. None of the faculty, for instance, had been used to full-time teaching. In the past they'd all mainly taught on the weekends in a setting that had seemed at once both more devotional and more casual. They also used more Arabic. Now there was a regular schedule, with expectations for a new kind of rigor and structure. Except in Arabic class, the language of the school was English, which, Omar said, had at times frustrated Imam Zaid and Sheikh Hamza, who'd both hoped there could be more Arabic memorization and reading in the classroom. They'd both had to readjust. Not only had Zaytuna decided early on that classes were going to be in English—"we've got to stick with the program," Omar had argued—but more to the point, the students were not ready yet for what Zaid and Hamza seemed to have in mind. Even for those students who had attended the summer Arabic course, their proficiency was not at a point that would lead to anything more than basic comprehension, if that, much less to understanding the subtleties of language that Hamza especially relied on in his discussion of words in general, but Arabic words—sacred words—in particular.

So with this in mind, Omar and the faculty had had to strike the right balance between imposing on the students' patience—the facilities, for instance, were still a work in progress; dormitory life had five men sharing one apartment—and insisting that they know Zaytuna intended to be "just as tough and rigorous" as any other college. No one here wanted a weekend school.

This meant that classes had to run more or less on time, giving some allowances for Muslim standard time. Quizzes announced for Tuesday would, in fact, have to take place on Tuesday. Students were to come prepared; beyond that their responsibilities would be laid out explicitly in Zaytuna's General Catalog: "To comply with course requirements . . . To take action to solve academic problems . . . To arrive in class on time . . . To take responsibility for the material covered . . . Not to have earphones or plugs in ears while on campus . . . ," and so on. Instructors had even more responsibilities still.

Blame it on homeschooling or blame it on being eighteen years old and away from home for the first time, but some of the younger students, in particular, Omar told me, were not ready for that structure when they arrived: "Their level of struggle is different."

Again, academically this struggle presented itself most obviously in Arabic, which also provided the obvious place to look to see differences among the students. Omar saw that the troubles many of them had with the language would force Zaytuna to reevaluate its expectations going in. The original plan, to move this first class through Arabic all at the same pace, simply wasn't going to work. Intermediate Arabic I was designed to include "readings in the Koran, hadith, and other primary classical sources"; it would introduce an "advanced level of vocabulary and grammar." At least six or seven students— that is, nearly half the class—weren't prepared for this. Omar's conclusion was that Zaytuna had probably asked too much of them.

And it had taken some time to realize this, which Omar described to me as a "just-in-time sort of thing." For these students, comparing themselves in the classroom to those more fluent than they had started to become overwhelming. And so, based on the feedback they got from students who had finally spoken up—a difficult proposition for struggling students in colleges anywhere, to say nothing of a place where you're taught by saints—the faculty came to the conclusion that moving forward they'd have to create an additional class to

accommodate two levels of proficiency. They'd considered the possibility of continuing to allow everyone to work together, but in the
end this, the faculty decided, would have held the more advanced
students back. After they'd made their decision, for the time being
the first-semester class had followed a more basic track; students who
were having a hard time were tutored in the evening by a teacher
from the Summer Arabic Intensive program named Yusuf Mullick,
who would himself find a teaching mentor in Dr. Hatem. Mullick
had then been hired on to teach full-time after the students returned
for the second semester. The group was split. The "more senior students," as Omar referred to them, would have a more project-based
class, which was meant to keep them challenged.

The root of the problem is that, on the whole, Arabic proficiency
among American Muslims is fairly low. Estimates from the Pew Research Center range from between 5 to 11 percent, or what Omar
called "low to none." "We need to build these students," he continued, before they can be expected to perform at a level that would
satisfy Imam Zaid or Sheikh Hamza. And yet, looking at models from
other colleges and universities, during the first semester the school
had also realized that those are probably not the best standard for
comparison. Success in Arabic language at UC Berkeley or Georgetown, say, as Zaytuna now saw it, would not be sufficient for what the
scholars here needed to be able to expect of their students in their
college. Looking ahead, Arabic would simply have to be one thing
that set the Zaytuna graduate apart. Whether the scholars might ever
be happy with the degree to which Arabic would play a role in their
history or theology classes—at least with this first class—Omar could
only speculate. His sense was that Zaid and Hamza would continue
to find they'd have to allow the students to "grow into the school."
They'd all only been at it a few months; perhaps by the second or
third year the scholars would be able to introduce more of what
they'd been hoping to. This would require patience, too.

For now, though, in addition to Mullick, there would be an additional Arabic professor at the school—a central hire they were considering to oversee the entire program. The new Arabic professor

would be responsible for overhauling the summer intensive program, as well, finding a way to integrate it more fully into the mission of the college. Beyond that, they were set on introducing a new Arabic course every year into the students' fourth year. They needed someone, Omar said, "to think only about Arabic. . . . That's the person we want." So far they'd received about thirty applications from around the country; of those there were five or six PhDs in the running.

Imam Zaid and Sheikh Hamza's proficiency—then fluency and eventually mastery—in the language had mostly come through immersion in the Muslim world. They'd each been gone for years. I asked Omar whether he thought four years of classes, mainly in English, would ever be enough.

"We don't know," he told me. "This is something where we need to walk in with our eyes open and ears open to see what we get." The stakes were high. "The proficiency we need to develop—the skills we need to develop in the students" must, he thought, make it possible "to go with Arabic texts. It's critical for us, because we need to create that differentiation of, 'Here, this is a Zaytuna graduate.'" Here was a tech guy, looking for the "better, different—faster, sleeker" student. "We have to have that value proposition showing in a graduate of Zaytuna."

What they would very much like to do is reach below them, as it were, into the high school and even middle-school level—something Hamza was already doing through his support of both Muslim homeschooling initiatives and Northstar, a K–eighth grade Islamic school founded in 2002 in the yurt on Zaytuna's Hayward campus. Members of the Zaytuna community, including Usama Canon and Imam Tahir Anwar, who sits on Zaytuna's Management Committee, had also been working toward the creation of Averroes Institute, an Islamic high school located alongside Ta'leef Collective in Fremont. (Averroes would open its doors in the fall of 2011.) Omar's sense was that part of Zaytuna's Arabic problem might be solved in the long term by working with preparatory schools like Averroes, and maybe "five or ten" others, he said. By helping them to develop an Arabic curriculum, Zaytuna might be assured that the students coming out of high school—those who decided to continue into Zaytuna College, at least—would simply be better prepared for what was ahead.

This also meant that looking ahead to future classes—"as people start to realize that we're here," Omar said, "as people become more familiar, more aware of this"—Zaytuna was counting on attracting more traditional undergraduate students, which meant more eighteen-year-olds and fewer master's degrees. The applications for year two were already bearing this out. And although Omar hesitated to say so, he also seemed to think this second class held slightly more promise coming in: "The types of applications we're receiving this year are actually much better than the ones from last year. And not to say that they were not good, but they are definitely stronger students, better students in some ways." Just by getting those doors open, Zaytuna seems to have convinced at least some part of the *ummah* that it was a real possibility for higher education. Omar continued, "I'm seeing a lot of parents who were probably skeptical last year at this time starting to think, or at least ask the question, 'So what are you guys doing? I'm thinking about my kid. Should he go there or not?' I think the questions are slightly changing, at least among the people who are close to us. I think the question they're asking now is, 'Is this a viable option or not?' Whereas before it was, 'No.'"

Faint praise, perhaps. But Omar would take it. "And I think in another year or two it will become more serious. And once we have the accreditation, if we can continue to maintain our standard, we will be a serious contender." In other words, for Muslims in this country who care about such things—and those numbers appear to be growing—Zaytuna, whose founders agree that all knowledge is sacred knowledge whose purpose is to bring us into a closer relationship with God, was offering parents something they couldn't find elsewhere. But this would mean, as far as Omar could tell, that those parents are "going to send their students here expecting a lot of things from us." And not just in Arabic or theology. "As far as general academia is concerned, we want our graduates to be just as recognized as any of the best schools in the United States. And they should be proud to say, 'I went to Zaytuna College.'"

And who would those students say such a thing to? I asked.

"I think it's everybody. It's the American Muslims. It's the United States of America. And it's the Muslim world. This is a high-quality Muslim education. . . . I think we have a lot to prove to a lot of people."

Of the problem Arabic had posed over the fall, I'd already heard a fair amount from the students. And the cohort, as Omar liked to call this first group of students, had already been split. Still, whatever adjustments Zaytuna had made in their other classrooms were nothing at all like what they'd had to do with Intermediate Arabic I. In English class, for instance, where, Omar offered, the students might have been getting a little bit bored early on, the instructor Shirin Maskatia had made the class more challenging. She'd anticipated the possibility before the semester even began: "I am providing you with a syllabus and a course description," Maskatia wrote, "based on my previous experience at Ohlone College. However, every class is different. As the semester progresses, I may vary class content and policies based on your needs and interests and on the goals of Zaytuna College."

One way this had happened over the course of the semester was in their writing about capital punishment. The students had wanted to think about the issue a little more from an Islamic perspective, which, Omar explained, necessarily changes the conversation. With a little push from the students, the laws of the land would come into contact with the laws of Allah. At the same time Maskatia was instilling in her students the principles of grammar and usage and argumentation, sentences and paragraphs, a bit of logic and rhetoric, she also offered an Islamic perspective on the topics at hand. And although Omar made clear that their decision to hire Maskatia was based on the credentials she'd built up over some thirty years of teaching—she has a PhD in English literature from Cornell—they'd also brought her on because "in the beginning it was just easy for us to tap into our own world." And when it's possible, tapping into their world is good, Omar explained, because too often core academic subjects—American history, in particular, he offered—have been taught from a perspective that has ignored or misrepresented minorities. And while there have, of course, been movements to correct this sort of bias in colleges throughout the country, Zaytuna was founded, in part, to offer an alternative perspective on American life that is rarely offered in our nation's classrooms.

While it's the case for now that all of the college's courses were being taught by Muslims, and it would always be that way for Arabic language and Islamic law and theology, Zaytuna's hope was different for what Omar called their "non-Islamic" classes. One of the advantages of opening the college in Berkeley would be to draw on scholars throughout the Bay Area, Muslim or not, to offer instruction in other liberal arts courses. These professors would be part-time; for the next three or four years, he supposed, the college wouldn't be able to make hires outside of its central disciplines. And yet, even in those cases, whether in critical analysis or American history, Omar's sense of the students was that they will make an effort, when necessary, to raise questions that will move the course in a particular, perhaps Islamic, direction. If the first semester had taught him anything, he said, it's that these students were very serious and committed to the program. "And when I've spoken with all of them," Omar continued, "I see that they have thought about this—why they wanted to come here." It was for God. "I think that they will certainly shine when they leave from here. . . . Many of them will be able to achieve significant things when they go out."

When I asked whether the size of the college or a lack of resources might keep Zaytuna from offering certain classes, Omar agreed that there were "some aspects of knowledge" that seemed too far afield for the school at this point. But above all else, in addition to Islamic law, theology, and Arabic, he stressed that Zaytuna would emphasize the "basic skills, the fundamental skills that a good, intelligent human being should have." Lessons in critical thinking, logic, research methods, and "rationalization," he said, would help prepare students for life as human beings, as much as what they might take away from a course in some subject the college had not yet planned for. "Once we build those skill sets, then they can go get the knowledge." As far as other subjects are concerned, Zaytuna had every intention of adding additional majors and programs, but somewhere down the road a bit.

For the time being, Zaytuna was a school centered entirely on God, approaching "education from a theistic framework, which provides a coherent perspective on the world," as its academic vision lays it out. While we talked, Omar put it even more simply: "Knowledge is knowledge, but you have to understand where it's grounded." Again, he meant all knowledge. "That's the right thing for us," he said.

He could speak only vaguely about Zaytuna's course offerings and the development of the "skill sets" associated with traditional liberal arts colleges, but he made this point: "If you still create that ability to critically analyze the information, then I think you're doing the right thing. And if God is at the center of it, then even better."

So, I asked, looking at the years ahead in a class on the US Constitution or perhaps a hard science, will it be difficult to reconcile what's taught in the liberal arts classroom with what's very obviously a religion class? My sense already was that Darwin's theory of natural selection would not go over well in a Zaytuna classroom. I knew Sheikh Hamza was of the opinion that denying intelligent design was completely mad. (In May he would give a speech where he'd declare that exactly, and follow it up by saying, "I don't care how many degrees you have. If you deny design in this world, as far as I'm concerned, you're a lunatic.")

Omar did not think this would be a problem. "In each class," he said, "a teacher has a lot of leeway as to how they want to teach the class." This meant that whoever would be teaching the US Constitution course or economics, for example, would bring to it their own understanding and expertise. Zaytuna College was not Zaytuna Institute: "It's not like Sheikh Hamza is teaching all the classes, where you're only going to get one perspective." Hamza would, however, be teaching astronomy, the lone science course Zaytuna had on offer as part of the degree requirements for the class of 2014. A major emphasis would be on moon sightings and calculating prayer times based on the traditional methods outlined in *fiqh*.

Zaytuna's next incoming class would be guided by a new vice president of academics, the key executive position I'd overheard Omar talking about the previous day. In his role as executive vice president, Omar had brought to Zaytuna the corporate, team-building savvy of a former senior manager at Microsoft; the new hire would have a PhD. At the moment, Dr. Hatem was the only permanent faculty member with a doctorate and a long, formative history as an academic. This would have to change. Where the new VP lacked administrative skills, Omar could lend a hand. "What we really need," Omar admitted, "is someone with an academic background . . . who can build a better academic environment."

The plan for the incoming class was to have no more than twenty new students. Fifteen might be better, but Omar worried about an arbitrary cap that might lock someone out that they needed: "So we might get a little bit greedy and say, 'This student, we've got to have him here.'" But based on what he'd observed from the first semester, fifteen is the right size. "If it's ten," he continued, "I'm actually happier, because it's more manageable than a class of twenty." Little did I know it then, but they'd all have a chance to test Omar's theory in the spring. Two of Zaytuna's first fifteen students would not be returning for the second semester. Dustin would leave after several weeks. If over the next four or five years they expanded at that rate—ten to fifteen new students per year, with some measurable attrition—they'd reach an enrollment of fifty or sixty students. "And that's plenty." Beyond that, they'd probably have to add new departments, which would expand the student base even more.

All of this would require more space, something their landlord, the American Baptist Seminary of the West, was well aware of. "As space becomes available, we'll take more space from them," Omar told me. In other words, he wanted to assure me, available space was not driving their admissions process. Regardless of how many students you enroll, he said, "you have to take care of them."

Omar had made this a personal commitment. He'd developed relationships with some of the students who had come to him with issues that always come up with first-year college students. "Life happens," he said: homesickness, the pressure, family. Imam Zaid and Sheikh Hamza had tried to step in where they could to take care of the students who needed their help. But in the future Zaytuna would have a dedicated chaplain. They already had someone in mind.

Before we left each other, Omar was pleased to tell me Zaytuna's library would finally be ready for the students to use after the new semester began. Just that weekend the painters would arrive. Then they'd roll out the carpets. Tables and chairs would be brought in after classes resumed. Student workers would line the shelves with books.

EIGHT

Peace Be upon Him

This is a college that we're starting from scratch. There
are going to be a lot of fits and starts. There will be a lot of
kinks. For example, the library: We're just getting the library
off now. And for an entire semester the students didn't have
a library on campus. But they patiently endured that.

—Imam Zaid

Now that there are books,
now that there are shops
selling books,
we come in to browse the stacks,

come looking for the spine
with "God" printed on it,
the tell-all the world wrote
in that sprawling hand.

—from "Book," by Rasheeda Plenty

I walked the halls of Zaytuna again, this time with Omar Nawaz's
right hand, the administrative assistant Ali Malik, on a Friday morning in early February. Fridays are usually quiet around campus; even
the administration keeps their calendars fairly open so that by around
noon they can begin making their way to *jummah* prayers.

Ali and I found Sumaya Mehai and Rasheeda Plenty shelving
books in the library, which was, as Omar had predicted, still very
much a work in progress. This was the first chance I'd had to see
the walls entirely lined with shelves; they were not yet entirely filled
with books. A few additional boxes of books had arrived from Sheikh
Hamza's home the day before, and the women had turned their attention to those. Unfortunately, their Arabic was not entirely up to

the task. With book after book they consulted with Ali to determine not only who wrote it, but what was the subject matter. Was it law? Ethics? A commentary? Where did it go?

I certainly didn't know. And yet, despite whatever confusion these ad hoc librarians felt in putting the books on the shelves, seeing them lined up with bright and gorgeous Arabic letters running together from volume to volume forming individual collections, this said something to me about Islam—something, I've often been told, many Muslims tend to forget.

Regardless of whether you read the Arabic, what constituted any author's body of work on those shelves is clear enough. That title begins on one book and ends ten or so books down the line. That's the work of one man. That's one piece of knowledge. Read it. Study it. And know that it represents just one perspective within a tradition filled with scholars. Placed one next to another, each collection announces itself by the script on its side as complete in and of itself; but it's impossible not to see the others lining up alongside, each announcing the very same thing: Read me.

Standing there admiring the scattered collections on the shelves, I was reminded of a class on the Koran I'd taken months earlier led by Sheikh Abdallah Adhami, onetime imam of Park51, held in the basement of the Church of St. Joseph in New York's Greenwich Village. On Saturdays the space is a soup kitchen. A blue AA meeting sign sometimes hangs near the door. Until recently, the New York University Islamic Center shared the space, as well.

That night, Sheikh Abdallah, who in nearly two hours managed to lecture on maybe three lines of the Koran, spending most of his time on the seemingly endless meanings and "implications" of the word "road," insisted and began to instill in me the idea that, in his words, "Islam is an oceanic tradition." The sacred knowledge possessed by any individual, he said, may be limited by his own humanity; and yet, there will always be a straight path for the Muslim, which the sheikh later referred to as the shariah, or the "vast road that leads to water."

Is it any wonder that he made the point about Islam being like the ocean? The shariah leads there. What's more, the road of the shariah is a strange sort of road that keeps the Muslim on it: the more you seek the vanishing point off in the distance, the more the road engulfs you. This is where the sheikh's metaphors—where Islam is the ocean and the shariah is the road—came together as one somewhat confusing whole; it wasn't clear why anyone might need a road when it's both as vast as the ocean and can swallow you up just as well.

The vastness of the tradition is meant to manifest itself in the individual Muslim, the sheikh continued. I was sitting on a folding chair behind students scattered on mats at his feet. One's own road into the faith, he said, will only be as vast as his mercy and generosity with others. One's ability to guide others depends on the person's willingness to be guided in the straight path himself. "Walk to Allah," Sheikh Abdallah concluded, "crawl to Allah, whether you are athletic, crippled, limping . . . come as you are."

Outside the library, when I asked Ali whether he'd be attending the afternoon *jummah* services at Oakland's Lighthouse Mosque, he replied, "It's Zaid! You gotta go, right?" He didn't, though, raise the possibility with Sumaya or Rasheeda. As we walked away back toward his office, he explained in hushed, embarrassed tones, that he never asks women about going to the mosque: "I don't know," he whispered, "whether they're on their menstrual cycle." This might, he said, keep them from the mosque for up to ten days.

Just then, sparing him additional embarrassment, Ali's phone buzzed with news from a friend.

"Dave Chappelle's in town," he said, looking up from his BlackBerry.

And in that moment the possibility of a real Islamic conspiracy became clear: each American city has a secret Islamic network that spreads the word when Muslim comic Dave Chappelle touches down.

I left Ali to his one remaining task of the morning, to try to arrange tickets for a few remaining students to an event called the Grand Mawlid, a huge celebration of speeches and performances honoring the birth of the Prophet, taking place that Sunday night at the Marriott in Santa Clara. Sheikh Hamza and Imam Zaid would both be speaking. On my way past the library Rasheeda and Sumaya told me they were wrapping things up; they would indeed be heading to the Lighthouse Mosque. We'd meet soon at the apartment the women shared and catch the bus with Leenah and Faatimah and Mahassin.

There was as much prayer and reading on the bus as there was talking. They all took turns, moving from bright conversation to silent reflection, but Faatimah especially was absorbed in the pocket Koran she carried with her and used, it seemed, to prepare for *jummah*. She also had taken to heart a lesson from the new Islamic law professor, old-time Zaytunie Sheikh Yahya Rhodus, who told them, "Always carry a little notebook around with you. Whatever inspires you, or rings true for you, was meant for you. So make sure you write it down." Faced with what Faatimah called the "obvious way" that the Zaytuna classroom—or really any classroom—was not like the rest of the world, and vice versa, every moment deserved the attention of a note-taker. Though the Zaytuna classroom might be structured with the books and schedules and tests that are the trappings of any classroom, what's "out here" is no less important, structured as it is, she said, "so much more obviously by the divine." The whole world is the classroom. She saw in it signs and proofs of Allah. Our ride to the masjid lasted some twenty minutes.

They were only a few weeks back into the routine of dorm living and classes, and reports were that things around campus felt both different and the same. The most striking difference was certainly the loss from classes of Abdul Jalil, Naeemah, and Dustin, although in Dustin's case he'd stuck around the Bay to continue his Islamic studies degree at UC Berkeley and to continue his courtship of Ala'. He'd moved out of the men's dorm, though, and was around less. Abdul Jalil and Naeemah had left town, reportedly back to Michigan, where they'd be getting married. Leenah was thrilled to be back in the Bay, which had felt like home from the very beginning.

Of course, I had to leave the women when we entered the mosque. Spotting Ali, I stepped in and made my way to kneel beside him. The mosque was packed, and before Imam Zaid could really get going with his sermon after the call to prayer, he asked the men in the front to make more space for the women, who, though in the same room, sat in several rows across the back wall. "Brothers, can you come forward? Pack in . . . pack in tight, you'll find mercy, *insha'Allah*," said Zaid. A natural path usually formed across the room, but given the numbers today that was disappearing. And unable to pack in any tighter, it quickly became clear that some of us—Ali and I included— were not long for the mosque.

The weather was beautiful and Ali and I marched out in our stocking feet with a number of the other men to take our places on the sidewalk. At the door some of the brothers laid a tarp over the concrete. Behind that, Ali spread out his jacket. We kneeled again on that. As was usual, Imam Zaid spoke into a microphone and today his message carried onto the street.

Zaid's sermon had opened in what he considered, "under the circumstances, in an unusual way," with a letter addressed to God by a twelve-year-old Pennsylvania girl whose father had been killed in the West Virginia Sago Mine explosion in 2006. Originally published in *USA Today*, the letter's closing lines represented Zaid's model of faith in times of calamity: "I love you God and I have never forgot that you are still in charge. I do understand why you did what you did. I love you daddy and God. Amen." This was a story Zaid often told.

Yet it's true, under the circumstances it hardly made sense to start this way. Here were those circumstances: Since January 25, just more than two weeks earlier, Egypt had been in revolt. That day, and for weeks to follow, Tahrir Square would be filled with revolutionaries. And just this morning it was announced that the dictator Hosni Mubarak had essentially been deposed. Still, whatever successes the revolutionaries achieved against the Mubarak regime did not come easy and, said Zaid, had been possible only because they'd responded to the message of the Prophet: "Respond with that which is best."

And you think you've got it bad, he seemed to be saying.

Zaid does not doubt or minimize the "many hazards" American Muslims face as they continue to "negotiate the future" in the United States. (The campaign-slogan hope of "winning the future" seems like too much to ask.) But, Zaid continued, those negotiations have not yet involved facing down hired "thugs" armed with "submachine guns and lances" or those "goons . . . charging horses and camels into a crowd." Those young Egyptians would not be turned back. By "holding on to the principle of unity, holding on to the principle of nonviolence," Zaid concluded, "they've been blessed to see the hold of the dictator released from them."

And then he pressed on. Even from outside the mosque you could feel a rising intensity, and Zaid brought his story of revolution back home. Back to America, back to North Oakland, to this storefront mosque spilling its congregation out onto Martin Luther King Jr. Way.

So many Muslims he knows, he said, are "tempted to turn back just because people are talking about them, just because people are looking at them funny, just because people are whispering when they walk by." And with a whisper he growled: "It's getting tense in America."

Then he played a character, the complaining and put-upon American Muslim: "They're talking about us. They're looking at us funny. Maybe I should abandon Islam. Maybe I should stop going to the masjid. Maybe I should take my hijab off. Maybe I should shave my beard. Maybe I should stop wearing my kufi. Maybe I should just"—he paused—"drift away."

Because with Zaid, the times do not call for assimilation, or the "Muslim stillness" Sheikh Hamza had spoken about. Today—and today was a "significant and symbolic day"—those drifters should find their inspiration in the history being made in North Africa. "But people of Egypt are showing that history isn't made by people who back down in the face of a challenge. History isn't made by people willing to compromise their heartfelt belief. History is not made by people willing to turn back at the first sign of trouble."

Zaid's mosque was filled with young people; what Ali had said at the doorway of Zaytuna's library seemed especially true for the Bay Area Muslims under thirty: "It's Zaid! You gotta go, right?" And today he'd made his entreaty for these local Muslims to make the kind of history the Egyptian revolutionaries had only just begun to forge in what would come to be called the Arab Spring.

. . .

After *jummah*, it was Imam Zaid, not Ali, who guaranteed my admission to the Grand Mawlid celebration that weekend. I did not have a ticket, I explained. No matter. If I had any trouble at the door, Zaid assured me, I should just call him.

That was my plan when I arranged to catch a ride to Santa Clara with the roommates Chris Cusano, Adnan Alam, and Haroon Imtiaz, who were borrowing a car and, as the hour to leave came and went, were running very late. They picked me up under the MacArthur BART station in Oakland, just blocks away from the Lighthouse Mosque, and we spent the next half hour driving around in hopes of finding a gas station. When I asked if Ali had arranged tickets for the women students as well, Haroon said, "If there's a mawlid, the sisters are going to be there!"

Adnan tried to make something of this remark, offering the complaint that the religious difference between men and women was something that was often talked about but never analyzed. Men they saw as more studious by nature; they filled Islamic schools and weekend seminars. Women had more enthusiasm. They were more emotional. Boys will be boys; girls, girls.

Once we found the gas station, Haroon, who had over the months often struck me as capable of getting lost in the world around him, struggled inside with an ATM while Adnan pumped the gas. Chris, who was dressed for the mawlid in a long white robe, stepped out of the gas station but couldn't, for whatever reason, locate the car right away. The whole thing reminded me of a Three Stooges film. In the driver's seat, giant, quiet Adnan played a kind of straight man. And yet, on the hour-long drive to Santa Clara, I thought Adnan would kill us all. He raced, dodging traffic on all sides. Time was against us. Dustin, who'd arranged other transportation, was keeping in touch with text messages: "We parking."

When we finally arrived, we met Dustin, who'd been lingering in the parking lot. Chris removed his pocket recorder from its case. Inside, we would split up during the mawlid itself. As the men went to find their seats, I was left to convince the women at the reception table that I was there as the guest of Imam Zaid. He'd told me to call him if there was any problem with my getting in, I explained. There was no problem.

Zachary Twist was there, and at the entry to the Grand Ballroom he handed me a small cup of water and told me it had come from a well called Zamzam near the Kaaba, the black cube building known as the most holy site in Islam. The well, he said, went back to the time of Abraham.

Zachary then found me a seat at a table of Zaytunies from back in the days of the Hayward yurt. As I settled in, onstage was Ali Ataie, a Muslim biblical scholar from General Theological Union who was performing a reading of the Hebrew Bible from an Islamic perspective. This was the theme for the celebration: "The Promised Prophet: Prophet Muhammad in the World's Scriptures." Sheikh Hamza, speaking at the end of the night, would spend some good portion of his presentation celebrating Muhammad by tracing the place of Islam through both the Old and New Testaments and then racing through a PowerPoint presentation about the Prophet's predictions about the end of time. Even racing, his talk would last ninety minutes.

Long before Hamza was scheduled to talk, dinner was served, and Imam Zaid took the stage with a sermon that first distinguished between praise and thankfulness. Praise was what this evening was about. It was the greater act. Zaid spoke with a kind of slow solemnity I had not heard in him before, a tone he reserved, it seemed, for discussions of the life of the Prophet. We praise, he told the crowd, not a particular gift, but rather the very fact that God is the giver of gifts. "Allah," he said, "has gathered us to praise his Prophet. . . . And we praise him because he is Muhammad." He's worthy, though, of much more than praise, said Zaid. Muhammad should also be seen as the "beloved," if only because Allah loved him: "One who loves someone loves those whom the beloved loves."

Zaid claimed he could not find the words to express what it was to love Muhammad, and so turned to the Koran: "'Say to them, O Muhammad, if it be that your fathers'—or your mothers, but he mentions the fathers," Zaid said. "'If it be that your fathers, your sons, your brothers, your wives, your clan, the wealth that you've accumulated, the business you fear declining, the dwellings you delight in, are more beloved to you than Allah and his Messenger and striving in His cause, then wait until Allah brings about his command, and Allah guides not a morally profligate people.' What more can be said?"

His solemnity had now grown into a rolling growl, and his voice cracked under the strain of the love he was describing. The imam was near tears: "What does the Prophet mean to us?" he asked. "Are we telling people about the Prophet? If we loved the Prophet we would never stop talking about him." He then called out: "Tell the world about our Beloved! Exemplify his character in our lives. Embody that character and strive for success, so that you can say, 'It's not from me; it's because I follow Muhammad.'"

And suddenly, just as Imam Zaid moved to the very end of his reflections, he returned to the approach I'd grown most familiar with, an engagement with the same world events he'd preached about in the masjid on Friday afternoon. But now, the "great, great event" that had begun in Tunisia had been just one of the many signs and proofs of the Prophethood of Muhammad. So had been the initial victory of the Egyptian people over their dictator.

Takbir!

Allahu akbar!

All the while Zaid was talking, I noticed children wandering the hall. During their talks, the scholars had all been projected onto screens off to the sides of the stage, and occasionally the cameras panned the crowd. One boy appeared on the screen playing a handheld video game, the screen bouncing light off his face. Fathers sat with children on their laps. Others in the room sent text messages. Even I was guilty: "Hey Mahassin," I tapped into my phone, "Scott here, enjoying my food! How about you?" At one point, I noticed Zachary Twist gesture playfully to his son, who had been chattering, to zip his lips.

Following dinner, Imam Tahir Anwar, from Zaytuna's Management Committee, took the stage: "Who would have imagined ten to fifteen years ago that we could bring together eleven to twelve hundred people to praise the Prophet!" He then introduced singers who would offer praises of their own. He asked for everyone's attention; please stop eating. Sheikh Rhodus, who'd recommended the students use notebooks, took the stage to offer his historical reflections on the beloved companion of the Prophet, the Persian Salman al-Farsi. He then offered a line of poetry that he tried to relate to the lives of contemporary American Muslims, especially converts like himself (and Salman): "Not everyone who becomes Muslim can we say becomes like Salman; he must become like Salman first, and then he will become a Muslim like Salman." What this meant was that the love of the Prophet requires that you, like Salman, "go through tribulations" for his sake.

One assumes that the tribulations Rhodus was referring to came, in part, as the result of Salman's being sold into slavery before being taken to Medina, where he met the Prophet and declared himself a Muslim. Salman also helped defend against a failed siege of Medina in 627, which became known as the Battle of the Trench. He recommended to the Prophet that they dig a trench around Medina to keep back an army of some ten thousand Jewish forces. As described in the Koran, this was a decisive victory for the Muslims: "And He drove down those of the people of the Book who backed them from their fortresses, and He cast awe into their hearts: some you killed and you took captive another part of them. And He made you inherit their land and their dwellings and their properties, and to a land which ye have not yet trodden, and God has power over all things."

"The end result"—and here Rhodus was talking about the end of time—"is for the people of piety."

Rhodus ended his speech with lines of poetry from Sheikh Hamza, and a poem called "Spring's Gift": "For me this world is not one jot / If I could simply be a thought." A thought of the Prophet, that is.

By the time Hamza took the stage after another video presentation, the crowd seemed exhausted.

Dustin joined us for the ride back to Oakland, which was less breakneck. And whether they were all inspired by the event—Hamza had been brought to tears describing the Prophet; "the most beautiful human being, and he would love everybody in this room," he'd choked—or excited to have returned to classes, the men's banter during the trip home was ebullient. I could barely keep up.

So far in the semester they'd had three sessions of Prophetic Biography; each class had brought Sheikh Hamza to tears. Those same tears had come to Hamza during that evening's mawlid, too, after running through any number of the prophecies contained in the hadith. Prophecy was verifiable. "If what he [Muhammad] says comes true, he is a true prophet," Hamza had said. "So let's see what he says." Each of the prophecies was about the end of times. And the audience had sat rapt, dazzled, it seemed, as much by the man speaking as the prophecies he preached about.

In one instance, Hamza had presented a slide of the Makkah Clock Royal Tower casting a shadow over the Kaaba, and said, "The Prophet said, 'You will see Arabs vying to build tall buildings.' The tallest building in the world is now in Arabia. . . . Now in Mecca, you see those tractors there; that was once a mountain. . . . 'The end of time won't come until mountains are removed from their places.'"

As we drove back from Santa Clara, Dustin explained that he'd used that same image with some young students he was tutoring, "to explain what modernity means."

Chris joked, "You're going to turn all your students into anti-modern Muslim hippies!"

For Hamza it had meant the end of days. Even so, the upshot of the entire night—if not everything Zaytuna was up to—was about the love of the Prophet and the future of the school. Hamza was "so passionate," said Dustin. "He has so much love for the religion. He's given his whole life to it."

The car buzzed with details of the Reviving the Islamic Spirit conference in Toronto, where Dr. Umar, Yemeni scholar Habib Umar bin Hafiz, Imam Zaid, and Sheikh Hamza had all been onstage together raising funds for the school. Women, they said, were placing gold jewelry on the tables in piles. Of the five hundred people in the room, four hundred had contributed something. Their college, they could say, was built by donations from North American doctors, not corrupt governments, which also reminded Dustin, at least, of the direct connection between the scholarships many of the students depended on and the community that had gathered in Toronto. We talked again about the pressure of those donations.

Hamza's keynote address at the Toronto conference had praised Wikileaks founder Julian Assange, and he'd followed up on this theme on a blog he writes as part of Sandala Productions, the sheik's online presence: "More leaks are said to come, and I for one am looking forward to it. It is good to see them squirm and scurry, as they feel, in their cockroach shadow lives, the light of the sun beginning to penetrate their subterranean worlds." Even given the context of the blog post, it's difficult to tell exactly whose "shadow lives" Hamza is referring to here; although, a conversation I had once with him about the 2010 anticorporate documentary *Inside Job* suggests he's referring to Larry Summers and Tim Geithner, representatives of the public sector, as much as Bank of America's Brian Moynihan. Hamza is no fan of late-capitalist consumerism. That is, perhaps, until he has to be, when it comes in the shape of those successful doctors and the women with their gold jewelry.

As Adnan steered us closer and closer to Oakland following the Grand Mawlid, I learned from the men about the near-death experiences that had led, in part, to Hamza's conversion. There were three car crashes. The police said he should not have walked away. Hamza had told his students of heat stroke he'd suffered in Niger after his conversion, about the malnutrition he endured in Mauritania, when he developed huge welts all over his body. And though Hamza relies on his own biography in his lectures and sermons, "none of us," said Dustin, "knows his life in full." He needed, they agreed, a "Malcolm X–like autobiography."

After 9/11, Hamza had risen into the halls of power. In Toronto, someone in the crowd had called him out for going soft ever since. From 2001 to 2004, Hamza traveled nonstop, they said; he would go to the international economic conference in Davos. Zaid had said at one point, "We need to be at the World Social Forum, not the World Economic Forum." He'd been called the true Renaissance man.

It was nearly one in the morning by the time we arrived back in Oakland. Haroon seemed to have been nodding off. Dustin and Chris could probably have kept going all night. Adnan dropped me where I was staying. I'd see them all soon, I said.

The next day, I checked my phone. In the early morning hours following the mawlid, Mahassin had sent me a text message in reply to the one I'd sent her during the dinner: "Lolololol!!!!!!" she wrote. "Just got your text. The food was delicious. I couldn't stop eating it even after Maulana [a scholarly title] Tahir suggested that we not eat during the singing."

It had come in at 2:38 a.m. Apparently, the women had been just as worked up after the mawlid as the men. Or vice versa, perhaps. The Prophet worked on them all (peace be upon them).

NINE

Sacred Caravan

I'm not really a spiritual progressive. I believe in treating
people well, but I don't believe in all this acceptance.

—Hamza Yusuf

Even reading the great books well is not an end in itself.
It is a means toward living a decent human life, the life of
a free man and a free citizen. This should be our ultimate
objective.

—Mortimer Adler

Most liberal arts colleges have some sort of honor code. Few strike
me as quite so conservative as Zaytuna's, which hangs on a bulletin
board in the lounge, where I waited for Ali Malik after attending an
early econ review with Dr. Hatem. It was now mid-March; the students were in the midst of their second-semester midterms.

According to the honor code, Zaytuna maintains as one of its guiding principles that the students must smell good. "Allah loves those
who purify themselves." Each of the code's six principles is supported
by a line or two from the Koran or a piece of hadith. The code also
requires personal accountability, timeliness (or again, affectionately,
"Muslim standard timeliness"), maintaining trusts, propriety and
modesty, and sobriety: "avoiding alcohol, tobacco, and mind-altering
drugs." There had never been, nor would there ever be, a kegger here.

I waited for Ali because early in the year Omar Nawaz had given
him the responsibility of arranging the right opportunity for me to sit
and talk at length with Sheikh Hamza. Midway through the school's
second term, this still hadn't happened. The truth is, unlike most everyone else around Zaytuna, Hamza wasn't yet especially clear about
who I was or what I was up to, sitting in on classes, showing up at
events where he was speaking, and generally hanging around. For

instance, I'd been in attendance just a few nights earlier when he was recognized by the liberal Jewish magazine *Tikkun* and what's called the Network of Spiritual Progressives, both cofounded by Rabbi Michael Lerner, for being "at the forefront of creating an Islam that rejects triumphalist interpretations and combines a traditionalist and mystical approach with an attentiveness to the religious and pastoral needs of the rapidly expanding Muslim community in the West."

I spoke that night with Munir Jiwa, of the Graduate Theological Union's Center for Islamic Studies, who with me took note of Hamza's late arrival to the event and then observed the appreciative crowd when the sheikh opened his remarks about mercy and justice and humility with a moving, tenor-pitched recitation from the Koran. The *Tikkun* event, held on the UC Berkeley campus, became for him another opportunity to challenge committed religious people like himself to acknowledge that there are people—"nutjobs," he calls them—who are "using our traditions" and "using the books that we use" and "using the words that we read," he said, and are "in so many places, causing so much harm." Denying this would be nearly as pathological as the triumphalism at the heart of Islamic extremism.

After the event, the sheikh was impossible to catch.

Of the three Zaytuna founders, Hamza remained the most difficult to pin down, although as the year went on Imam Zaid had begun to seem nearly as elusive. Since the opening of the college the demand had only increased for the founders to lecture and raise funds for both Zaytuna and an ever-growing number of other North American Muslim institutions, from local, nascent elementary schools like Zachary Twist's Northstar and Hamza's sister's homeschooling outfit, Kinza Academy, to such well-established organizations as the Islamic Networks Group (ING), the Islamic Society of North America (ISNA), and, of course, the Toronto conference, Reviving the Islamic Spirit (RIS). Introducing Hamza at his event, Rabbi Lerner declared that he'd been the only Jew among ten thousand Muslims at RIS. He then corrected himself; his wife had gone, too. These men were staples everywhere around the country. And there was the international travel, too, though this had always been more the case for Hamza than for Zaid. The travel—Hamza's simply being away so much—had been one of the motivating factors behind Zaytuna's need for the structure and institutional grounding that becoming a college promised.

We were just one day before Hamza's next trip, in fact, a point Ali made when he arrived in the lounge. He'd be missing two full weeks of classes. So, about my finally sitting down with Hamza, Ali said, it would again be tough to find the time.

The students were now all waiting in the classroom for Hamza to arrive to teach. Ali and I waited, too. It might be easiest, Ali reasoned, to arrange time with him if we caught him in person.

We would have no such luck.

A call came in just minutes after class was supposed to have begun, which sent Ali into a sort of panic—both for my sake and for his. Hamza wasn't coming. He had too much to do before his trip. The sheikh would be leading a group of Muslims to Mecca and Medina to perform *umrah*, or the "visitation." Compared with the hajj, the journey to the cities of the Prophet that all Muslims must make at least once in their lives, *umrah* is known as the lesser pilgrimage. For Hamza, this was a yearly commitment organized by Sacred Caravan, an organization based in Fremont, California. Muslim pilgrims can travel alone or join the group in its travels for an all-inclusive cost of about $3,500. Note well: "All sisters traveling under the age of 45 must be accompanied with a Mahram," an adult male chaperone.

Sheikh Hamza's flight to Jeddah would leave the following afternoon. Our interview would again be delayed. *Unless*—Ali put his hand over the mouthpiece of his BlackBerry: What if he could arrange for me to drive Sheikh Hamza to the airport?

Sure, I nodded. Ali hung up the phone.

As for the students all still waiting for their teacher? Ali's solution would follow the pattern set by liberal arts colleges across this great land: When the teacher doesn't show up, the students watch a video.

Like his first-semester class in theology, Hamza's Prophetic Biography class met once per week, this term on Wednesdays; and again, the students would rush to this class and find opportunities to quote from it in conversation or make references to Hamza's lectures in their social networks. Facebook was abuzz with lines from class; Tumblr contained dictated notes. Faatimah, for one, had found inspiration in Hamza's lecture about the wisdom of the Prophet's first wife, Khadija, the world's "second Muslim." In class, Hamza had lectured on the occasion when the Prophet first received the revelation from the angel Jibril, or Gabriel; Khadija knew immediately what the Prophet himself did not—that this revelation was from God.

The Prophet had rushed home, Sheikh Hamza said, and Faatimah recorded his every word as best she could: "He ran out of fear and confusion. He did not recognize Jibril's angelic reality; he only witnessed his majesty, and fled from its overwhelming presence. He came to his refuge, Khadija, and implored her to cover him, embrace him, wrap him up so tight that he would no longer feel the assault of grandeur's confusion. So tight that his heart would feel safe enough to stop leaping in his chest. So Khadija did just that because their relationship was such that his desire was her inclination before asked. He placed his head on her chest and their two hearts exchanged something in confidence. The Prophet was distressed to find that Jibril was still there—his awe filled the horizon. So she gently placed his head on her lap, but Jibril was still there. Then she took the scarf that covered her hair and placed it elsewhere. At this Jibril fled. A dignified, ennobled and modest being, he would not stay in a place in which a man and his wife were having an intimate moment. Khadija knew this, but the Prophet did not. She knew that a satanic presence would linger as she progressed in her calculated actions, but a being of beautiful grace like Jibril would leave them to themselves. Calculated though it was, love was her impetus, means and end. The Prophet was blessed to have such a wife."

When I later asked Faatimah what she took from the lesson that day, she described Hamza's delivery as a virtuosic musical performance; he "did something akin to what a master guitarist does to a guitar—he made it sing; he made it cry." Yet for her, the music of Zaytuna had been playing all along, with the scholars testing the strings—"putting us in tune," she said—always comparing the notes of the students, their increasing knowledge, to "the fine tuning of their own instrument." During the sheikh's lesson about the Prophet and Khadija, Faatimah recalled, there was finally the sense that when "he said 'Khadija and Muhammad,' 'Muhammad and Khadija,' we hit the right note." For Faatimah's part, when Hamza spoke about Khadija and the Prophet, the story finally came to life—indeed, "larger than life." She told me: "When he spoke of Khadija and our Prophet I saw a woman who moved, and a man who moved with her. For the first time I wanted to know everything about her from the curvature of her lips when she smiled to whether she closed her eyelids fully when she consoled the Prophet or if she rested her gaze upon him as he rested his head upon her chest. I wanted to close my eyes and see if I could remember the details of her face the way a child who has lost her mom yearns for the fading image of her mother. She became to me, larger than life at that moment. I felt I had some understanding as to why God planned him for her and her for him."

Muhammad and Khadija had four daughters, and the Prophet's favorite was named Faatimah.

While Sheik Hamza's students watched the video on the life of the Prophet, I sought out Maryam Kashani. Maryam was still busy conducting video interviews with the students as part of her PhD work at the University of Texas. And it had finally happened, she agreed as we spoke that day, that after the shock and surprise of finding themselves each day in classes with the likes of Imam Zaid and Sheikh Hamza, the students seemed to have settled in. I wasn't the only one to see that for those students who had returned for the second semester, Zaytuna had become home.

Leenah and I had discussed getting together after Sheikh Hamza's class, and so Maryam and I met up with her near campus after the video wrapped up. We'd join Mahassin and Rasheeda at Cafe Intermezzo, a popular Berkeley haunt that served up enormous portions (it has since burned down). Walking alongside Leenah on the way to Intermezzo, I asked how classes were going.

"Grammar is getting funner," she said. Obviously she meant Arabic.

The women would end up taking home more of their sandwiches than they ate that day. And what I learned over lunch was that so far,

the spring term had been a busy and productive time for the Zaytunies, particularly outside the classroom. The winter break seemed
to have given the students an opportunity to reflect on what had become of them over their first semester, but had also prompted them
to begin forming themselves into both permanent and ad hoc organizations that might prove useful both to them and the class they had to
imagine coming in behind them. Those seemingly far-off newcomers
were now a regular consideration.

To succeed, Zaytuna would have to grow, and since early in the
year these first students had been welcome spokespeople for the
school. Haroon and Chris had appeared in short autobiographical
videos posted online and sent around by Zaytuna to a mailing list
comprising mainly funders and communities of prospective students.
The series of videos was titled *Continue Your Story*, and was obviously
meant as an appeal to future applicants. A video by Michigan native Abdul Jalil ibn Abdul Halim, one of the three or four Zaytunies
who'd kept their distance from me and one of the three who hadn't
returned for the second semester, was titled *Detroit Steel*. A few of
the women led online information sessions for prospective students,
where, in late February, for instance, Leenah described Zaytuna as
just "too good to be true" and Faatimah declared that so far the experience had "fulfilled every hope" she had.

There was a similar kind of writing on a new Zaytunies blog
called *Let God*, which began with a reflection by Rasheeda, still the
school's resident poet. "Bismillah" (in the name of God), she began,
and then proceeded to narrate, with an imagination stretching back
to the Prophet himself, how over three years studying Arabic in the
summers, she'd discovered "a startling love"

> that crowded my heart (to the point of rupture, it felt sometimes)
> with my teachers and classmates, the people I met and came to
> know . . . that made me understand (in my small capacity) how
> the Companions loved the Prophet, may God send peace and
> blessings on his illuminated being, how his face was like the full
> moon, like the sun to them, to us. And our Prophet loved God,

with a vastness and depth that pulled us all in, that showed us how
to love God and each other.

"And please," she concluded, "keep all of us students in your
prayers and duas." ("Duas" are prayers of supplication.) Then: "God
is Greater."

You name it; God is greater.

Faatimah followed up on the blog a few days later, describing a certain "disconnect . . . just short of devastating" she felt as
a younger woman when confronted with the idea that a language
could remain unintelligible yet be so overwhelmingly meaningful—
"foreign to my tongue and yet familiar to my heart"—while also
"gently command[ing] my limbs into submission." This was the Arabic she'd come to Zaytuna to learn. The Arabic she pores over with
delicate hands on the bus, worrying her pocket Koran. Head down,
she's studying.

At times apparently overcome by her spiritual life, by the life of
the Prophet, by the life of Khadija, Faatimah can seem the most se-
rene and self-possessed of the women, composed to the point of stillness. She's the most easily brought to tears. And she usually has the
easiest and biggest laugh.

There were also bylaws in the works for a student government,
headed up so far by Rasheeda and Jamye and Veronica. Zaytuna's
Muslim Student Association had been organized in recent months—
though I had to wonder why such a thing was even necessary—and
one Friday in the middle of March they joined MSAs from UC
Berkeley and Dartmouth for lunch at a local restaurant called Julie's,
jummah services at the UC's Hearst Gymnasium, and a program to
distribute brown-sack lunches to the city's homeless. They went to
People's Park, across the street from Zaytuna's campus. The weather
was terrible; hail piled up. They fed maybe fifty people with peanut
butter and jelly.

What Adnan witnessed was trauma. Thinking back on his day with
the Dartmouth students, who seemed to know so much more than he
did about inequality and poverty, he wrote on the blog, "Some of the

people we met at People's Park had suffered from abuse in their past, while others were dealing with the fears that come from being homeless and hungry. These powerful experiences often elicit powerful emotions and people struggle to cope with these emotions as best they can." Still, it was clear by the way Adnan composed his reflection that Imam Zaid, whose own speeches and sermons and writings are often perfect knots of civil rights and black power rhetoric, had gotten through to him. The message had started with Zaid's mother, the late Richelene Mitchell, and was passed down to the little boy Ricky; today it was being transmitted in that chain from the grown man Zaid Shakir to his student Adnan Alam. The words sound very much the same. The world has produced "tribulation and trauma," said Adnan after his time with Berkeley's homeless; our "modern culture and the body politic," he continued, "revolves around exploiting fear, uncertainty, or doubt." From Jim Crow to Islamophobia to the disdain for immigrants, foreigners, and our nation's poor, whatever solutions there were to our country's sins required developing "countermeasures to these emotions"—fear chief among them—that may "have the unintended consequence of defanging many of the world's bigots, chicken-hawks, and demagogues."

The Zaytuna hero Malcolm X had answered much the same way when interviewed in 1965, after adopting traditional Islam; his influence is clear. His countermeasure? "I don't worry. I tell you, I am a man who believed that I died twenty years ago and I live like a man who is dead already. I have no fear whatsoever of anybody or anything."

A Zaytuna student-teaching program was in the works, as well, designed to prepare the older students to mentor the classes coming up behind them, and so on over the years, filling a gap this inaugural group had faced when they started without anyone really to look up to—except perhaps each other. Imagine entering college without any sense—or worse, without any example—of what was to come or what would be expected of you. And despite the regular encouragement they received, with Sheikh Hamza or Imam Zaid at the front of the room—or any other of the teachers, really, but mostly those two—classes could be intimidating. No matter that they tried never

to take personally whatever small pangs of inadequacy they sometimes felt when being corrected in the classroom. Indeed, recalling
those moments especially, perhaps, the students tended to express a
certain gratitude for having the opportunity at all. And while they all
felt grateful when the year began, for those who stuck it out into the
spring, this attitude seemed only to increase. "Thank you, Allah,"
Rasheeda has said, "for placing me here." When viewed this way—as
seems to be the case more often than not among the students—a
red mark on an essay or Arabic grammar quiz becomes a lesson of
the heart. But those lessons always came with the added pressure
of being the first people to attempt this—they were making history, Imam Zaid had said time and again—and the awareness that
their individual successes as students were essential if the school itself were ever to last into the following year. And where the school
and their situation as the "historic" first class called for it, they were
attempting—sometimes on their own—to meet the needs of those
whose applications were just now rolling in.

To start, Rasheeda had taken on the role of mentoring Leenah,
who, when describing how Rasheeda had first raised the possibility,
made the whole opportunity seem like the most wonderful honor
she'd ever received. Over lunch at Intermezzo, Leenah was near tears
when she explained the gravity and sincerity with which Rasheeda
had offered to be her mentor. Would she like some official guidance
and the opportunity to teach in the fall?

When I later asked Imam Zaid about this program during a public online open house with prospective students, he denied knowing
anything about it: "I think that's an unsubstantiated rumor. Maybe
some of the advanced Arabic students might be helping out, but as
far as I know, I wasn't standing under that part of the grapevine, so I
didn't catch that particular rumor."

We took separate cars, with Ali leading the way to Sheikh Hamza's
house in San Ramon. Ali drives fast, so I tried to stay close. We met
Sheikh Hamza's sister Nabila and his mother Elizabeth out front; the
sheikh's five boys streamed out behind them, as well, into the court-
yard between the house proper and the outbuilding Hamza uses for

prayers. The kids roughhoused with Ali, who took the smallest ones over his shoulder for a ride.

I'd arrived driving a black BMW SUV I'd borrowed from a friend who lives in the Bay, and I was wearing a white shirt, black tie, and dark slacks, which maybe explained why Nabila at first mistook me for the help—a chauffeur, as it were, for her brother; she'd seen it plenty of times before. Unlike Ali, I wasn't someone the family knew. Directed to their luggage, then, I decided simply to do my part loading it into the back of the vehicle while we waited for Hamza and his wife, Liliana, still out running last-minute errands. A few of the older boys would go along on this trip and ride with Ali to the airport. The youngest would stay behind with Hamza's mother and sister and her kids. Ali had arranged it so that Hamza and Liliana would ride with me.

Piling the last few bags into the car, Ali and I explained to the women that I hadn't actually been hired for the day, though I certainly didn't mind lending a hand. With Hamza's five boys and Nabila's children there, too, the household was chaotic. In any event, I was there to talk with Hamza about Zaytuna, I explained, and this resulted in our all removing our shoes and making our way into the house. We'd wait for him there.

The front room of the house had little furniture to speak of; there were rugs covering the floor. I sat with Nabila and Elizabeth on a sectional couch in a room off the dining room where the family watched videos. Elizabeth was mainly quiet; she'd apparently not been altogether well lately. A convert in the model of her brother, Nabila talked with me about homeschooling, the focus of Kinza Academy, which she founded in 2001. Mainly a developer of home-education curricula for Muslim families, Kinza has on its advisory board both Hamza and his brother Troy, in addition to former New York public school teacher and education activist John Taylor Gatto, whom Nabila credits with shaping her ideas against compulsory public education. The year she founded the school, Gatto was gaining traction as a reformer with his book *The Underground History of American Education: A Schoolteacher's Intimate Investigation into the Problem of Modern Schooling*. He appeared that year on a panel organized by *Harper's Magazine* at New York's New School for Social Research, where he maintained that American public schools were operating essentially as factories, producing "wonderful fits for the economic machine." His conclusion: "We have been *schooled* to have no inner life at all." By 2003, this time writing in *Harper's*, his point was sharper still: "We must wake up to what our schools really are: laboratories of experimentation on young minds, drill centers for the habits and attitudes that corporate society demands. Mandatory education serves children only incidentally; its real purpose is to turn them into servants. Don't let your own have their childhoods extended, not even for a day." It was Gatto's urgency—an obvious quality in Hamza's home, as well, and in his five homeschooled boys—that Nabila impressed upon me as we spoke.

When Hamza arrived home he went immediately upstairs to shower. When he returned, he leaned in to check in with his mother—"How have you been feeling?" he asked—and then seemed to be gathering his thoughts before we left. We didn't say much, though one thing he noted while we waited for Ali and Liliana to get everything situated in the cars, was that the full-body massage chair in the corner essentially went unused, but that since it had come as a gift from a follower, and was presumably quite expensive, he'd had to keep it. As we moved to the cars, he remembered hearing that the forecast was for unseasonably cold weather in Saudi Arabia. Liliana went back in to get him a sweater, which, along with a children's toy car, he would end up leaving behind in the backseat of the BMW in the rush to make the plane.

One thing you learn quickly in conversation with Sheikh Hamza is that like most religious conservatives, he does not like pornography. And he's hardly shy about it; studying and preaching against the social costs of "perverted, excessive, or deficient" desires has been a kind of pet project for him in recent years. Indeed, the problem was preoccupying him as he climbed into the BMW, complaining to me about the introduction of the dot-XXX Internet domain he'd recently read about, which a Florida entrepreneur named Stuart Lawley first proposed as early as 2005. (Sale of these domains would begin in December 2011.) If nothing else, he said, the domain "opens up a massive can of worms for kids," who would need to know nothing more than these three letters to find a whole separate Internet essentially run by the obsessive-compulsive Shaytan.

Hamza has often spoken on the topic, usually with reference to a paper he first presented at Princeton in December 2008, "Climbing Mount Purgatorio: Reflections from the Seventh Cornice." The three epigraphs to the essay, whose title already invokes Dante, come from Shakespeare, Pope, and Nietzsche, which is in keeping with Hamza's ecumenical "great books" approach to his writings and lectures, and even the conversation we were about to have, which would bounce from *Othello* to Stephen King, and from Goethe and Heidegger to Marx and David Foster Wallace, the brother-in-law, he said, of his brother's best friend.

The next few paragraphs of that pornography paper call on Plato and Rumi and Spinoza, and by the end he will have trotted out more than two dozen other classical and modern thinkers—from his Muslim heroes Ahmad Zarruq, Ibn 'Arabi, and Imam al-Ghazzali to W. H. Auden, Mortimer Adler, Joni Mitchell, and Bob Dylan. Presumably none of them have liked pornography much either.

From the Islamic tradition, in his argument Sheikh Hamza draws on the notion that within us is something known in Arabic as the *nafs*, what I've otherwise had described to me as the "lower self," but what he calls the "ego" or, left to its own devices, our "tainted soul." The quintessential struggle of the Muslim—what's often understood as the greater jihad—is to command the *nafs* such that we tame and refine, as he puts it, the "source of our special nature and distinction among other creatures." But, writes Hamza, given our own passions, the world's illusoriness, and once again, "an obsessive and compulsive force referred to as Satan (*Shaytaan*), which according to the Prophet Muhammad, flows in the very arteries of men and women," the *nafs* threaten to be "the single most destructive force in our world." And we're often most susceptible, especially when bored and alone in front of a television or computer screen, to the most basic and essentially selfish pursuits of the *nafs*: sensual pleasure. We watch porn. And it's destroying us.

What will save us? The same thing that's always saved us from ourselves. "Chastity," Hamza writes, "while far too often perceived as an antiquated 'woman's virtue,' has been a steadfast guardian of human well-being and an effective restraint from falling into the potentially bottomless pit of lust and wantonness." Hamza's great worry—to say nothing of his annoyance—about the dot-XXX Internet domain was that this bottomless pit he'd written about could be opened from any web browser.

With this, we began our drive to the airport. From the backseat over the next forty-five minutes, Liliana would balance assorted paperwork and a series of phone calls while also offering me directions to San Francisco airport. Hamza would first quiz me for several minutes about why again I was driving him to the airport and what it was I was doing around Zaytuna. When I answered with passing reference to Fox News commentator Frank Gaffney, who in 2009, recall, warned of Zaytuna's role in a "stealth jihad in America," Hamza compared him to Iago, that troublemaking, demonic figure who sews dissension and "cannot stand the idea of tolerance." Here's also where Stephen King came up, in a brief digression into the film version of his novel *Needful Things*, which features Max von Sydow as the proprietor of a new antiques shop in the town of Castle Rock, Maine, who by way of various bits of mischief manages to destroy the town from within. Von Sydow's character, Leland Gaunt, is revealed in the film to be the devil, which was cause for Hamza to point out the actor's range; he'd also played Jesus Christ in *The Greatest Story Ever Told* (as well, of course, as Father Merrin in *The Exorcist* and Ming the Merciless to Sam Jones's Flash Gordon).

And so we were on our way. To that most basic question about his life and his grounding in the Muslim world, Sheikh Hamza pointed me to Scott Kugel's book on Ahmad Zarruq, the first chapter of which is about him: "If you want to get the very best thing, it's pretty much a summary of what I'm about . . . I couldn't have done a better job. It kind of blew me away when I read it, and I don't even know the guy." And though Hamza would say, on the one hand, that Zarruq "was a much greater scholar than I could ever be," on the other hand, he claims to have given the Sufi saint a new life in the modern world: "He wasn't that well known," he said. "I turned a lot of Arabs on to him."

What this means is that for Hamza, rejuvenating the Islamic past in this country likewise involves more than indulging nostalgia. His point in helping to establish the liberal arts curriculum at Zaytuna, the piece of the school he's least ambivalent about, is part of a larger ambition to bring the sacred knowledge he gained throughout the Muslim world into conversation with classical texts of the Western tradition. Things he is more ambivalent about include lessons he's taken from his sister's mentor John Taylor Gatto, about moving from his "freestyle" approach at Zaytuna Institute, which looked a lot like what he'd done in West Africa, and seeking official accreditation from an educational establishment. He's not at all keen on grades. He despises textbooks and would never use one. He's not sure, either, whether the three founders agree fundamentally about the school's basic educational philosophy. "I'm not entirely clear myself," he said. "I definitely have the big picture, but the details and fleshing that out takes a lot of time and thought. And I'm not totally sure I'm on the same page as Dr. Hatem. We come from very different worlds. And he's actually very left. I'm pretty conservative. Even though I come from a leftist background, from my mom's side. But I'm actually conservative."

It's also clear to him why other conservatives—some not so ideologically different than he is—"hate academia"; they know that so much critical theory is a version of Marxism that's totally detached from the kind of classical training Marx himself relied on. And what's more, for many of those who study with Hamza at the Graduate Theological Union, where he's finishing a PhD, the application of Marx in specific varieties of religious studies doesn't take into consideration the fact that his theories were, he says, "hell-bent on destroying those religious traditions."

Putting classical texts at the core of a liberal arts education is a lesson he takes from his father David Hanson, a student of the legendary Columbia professor and great-books pioneer Mark Van Doren, another of Sheikh Hamza's intellectual heroes. (Hamza, whose first name was originally Mark, was named after Van Doren.) He claims that part of what he contends with in carving out a place between the Frank Gaffneys of the world and what he calls the "bizarre, idiotic, literalist mind" of extremists of all stripes—though religious extremists especially, and Muslim extremists in particular—is the denial or basic rejection of the past. For extremists on both sides, the core of Islam's history looks to the rest of us like dark barbarism: on the one hand, it's the often-vicious striving for purity in the name of Allah, and on the other it's the fear that those strivings are present in the heart of every Muslim.

With the world the way it is, Hamza told me, seeing such dark barbarism isn't totally unreasonable. And at this point in the conversation, he was as frank as I'd ever heard him be: "I just think religion is an insane—" He paused. "It's just that there are so many ways that it can go wrong. And it works with people who are already balanced. But when you get people that aren't balanced, and there aren't people to help them—" Again he paused. *Well*, Hamza seemed primed to say, *that's when you get trouble.*

TEN

The Citizen

You have a good example in Abraham and those who followed him. They said to their people, "We disown you and the idols which you worship besides God. We renounce you: enmity and hate shall reign between us until you believe in God only."

—Koran 60:4

Sometimes standing for the truth means standing against the Muslims.

—Hamza Yusuf

When Sheikh Hamza appeared at New York's Cooper Union in 2008 for his public conversation with Temple University's Khalid Blankinship, the two men were offering what they believed would be a guide for Muslims to faithful American citizenship. Both men seemed equally committed in their remarks to either side of an equation that for Christians in this country often feels like second nature: faithfulness is Americanness. And though Hamza believes it can be—and Zaytuna, he hopes, will make it so—for many Muslims, the equation doesn't feel natural at all.

This is not only, the scholars would say, because American Muslims have been largely misunderstood and ill-treated in recent years, although there's no denying that. (Both Imam Zaid and Sheikh Hamza point out that if you really want to see Muslims being dealt bad hands, just take a look throughout the Muslim world. As Hamza has told me, "A lot of these young Muslims born here are not always aware of the history of real persecution of other communities. They would do well reading more history.") What often makes American citizenship difficult for Muslims is a fundamental question concerning permissibility, according to Islam, to live in non-Muslim lands. On the big, broad strokes—about the unity of God and the unique status of Muhammad, say, and the requirements to pray, give alms, fast, and perform the hajj pilgrimage—there is widespread agreement. But the devil, as they say, is in the details. That day with Blankinship, Sheikh Hamza reminded the audience that Muslims have always disagreed more than they've agreed—including on this point of participation and allegiance as a citizen of a non-Muslim country.

The debate over Muslims living in non-Muslim lands had "raged," Hamza said, even in the early days of Islam. And as Muslims over their history lost lands to conquerors—the Mongols, say, in the thirteenth century—or in regular conflict with Christians, the debate persisted and intensified. At issue have always been the risks involved in either not being at complete liberty to practice Islam outside the Muslim world, or, as UCLA's Khaled Abou El Fadl has suggested, in the possibility that "a Muslim could inadvertently contribute to the material strength of non-Muslims which could then be used against Muslims." And yet, Hamza claimed, of the four great imams, only Imam Malik, the namesake of his own *madhhab*, deemed it impermissible for a Muslim to live outside a Muslim-majority territory, which if nothing else indicates the real diversity of valid and respected opinions on the matter—to say nothing of Hamza's own disagreement with jurists of his chosen school of thought. After all, although God knows best, he said, even members of the Maliki school believe it's acceptable to perform *dawah*, or promote the faith, in non-Muslim countries. How can you spread Islam in a place where you cannot also live Islam?

For his part, writing about the legal discourse on Muslim minorities, Abou El Fadl would also note that the Hanbali school of jurisprudence was more aligned with the Maliki school than Sheikh Hamza let on in his discussion at Cooper Union, and that it's probably more accurate to say that the four great imams were split fifty-fifty on whether it was permissible for Muslims to live in a non-Muslim land. Hanifi and Shafii jurists have historically offered what Abou El Fadl calls the "most sophisticated responses to the question." He would also point out, however, that although the Koran itself "does not command Muslims to live in Muslim territory," even the most sophisticated of Islamic juridical rulings must meet the eternal requirement "that people conduct their affairs according to God's revelations." Determining where in the world this is possible, Abou El Fadl argues, has been "redefined, rearticulated, and recast" over the centuries. Today these things are happening by the very fact of Zaytuna College—an institution trying to establish roots here and indigenize the faith, as they say—as Sheikh Hamza and his colleagues commit in the classroom to America's other three R's.

That day with Professor Blankinship in New York, Hamza quoted one piece of the hadith that says, "Establish your prayer, pay your zakat, avoid all foulness and live wherever you want to live." This sounds a little like Saint Augustine's *"Dilige et quod vis fac,"* or "Love and then what you will, do." The sheikh then quoted what he called a weaker, less verifiable, report of the Prophet: "The whole earth is God's earth. . . . Wherever you find good you can live there." As with Augustine, the more strongly attested of the narrations from Muhammad seems to ask more of the Muslim than of the land in which he or she lives or the people who rule that land. It's never up to the rest of the world to be good. With the Prophet, you must pray, you must give, and you must avoid sin. With Augustine, it's somewhat more simply put, but the message is strikingly similar: You must love. Once those things are in place, then what you will, do. So long as you're free to pray, give, and love, it doesn't matter where you are.

And yet, at the same time, Hamza believes it does matter where you are. Or, at least it matters where he is. And as we proceeded to the San Francisco airport that day in March 2011 so that he could once again make the lesser pilgrimage with his family and a host of his followers, Hamza was considering that debate once again—with me—about the permissibility of calling this country home.

Earlier that day, the *New York Times* posted online the cover story for that week's Sunday magazine, "Why Yasir Qadhi Wants to Talk about Jihad." This was another in a string of in-depth articles by *Times* reporter Andrea Elliott, who in recent years had written another cover story for the magazine, "The Jihadist Next Door," about Alabama native Omar Hammami, a convert who moved to Somalia to join an Islamist guerilla army known as al-Shabab. The Shabab,

Elliott reported, was linked to al-Qaeda. Elliott's March 2006 series
for the *Times* about the Egyptian-born Sheikh Reda Shata and his
storefront mosque in Brooklyn won her a Pulitzer Prize. Hers was
"the story of Mr. Shata's journey west: the making of an American
imam." (Not long after Elliott's reporting on Shata, he moved from
Bay Ridge, Brooklyn, to Middletown, New Jersey, to head Masjid Al-
Aman, where, according to the *Times*, he "now leads doctors, lawyers
and engineers in the five daily prayers." No longer in a storefront,
Shata's congregants are mainly prosperous Egyptian immigrants who
have been in the United States for decades.)

Yasir Qadhi has a far greater profile among American Muslims
generally than Sheikh Reda, as he is known. A Yale PhD candidate,
resident scholar at the Memphis Islamic Center, and dean of Academic Affairs for AlMaghrib Institute, an educational organization
that teaches Islamic theology mainly during weekend seminars, Qadhi is perhaps as well known in the United States as Sheikh Hamza.
He's younger, though, and while American-born, a Texan, Qadhi is
not a convert. And because he inclines more than Hamza toward a
literalist reading of the Koran and also because, as Elliott highlights,
"a handful of AlMaghrib's former students have heeded the call" to
violence—including Umar Farouk Abdulmutallab, the 2009 Christ-
mas Day "underwear bomber"—Qadhi has drawn the attention of
law enforcement officials in recent years. (Writing in October 2010,
Qadhi remembers his one encounter with Abdulmutallab as "so brief
and dull, that when I saw his pictures being paraded on every website
and news magazine cover in December of 2009, I didn't even recognize him.") Though he calls his own approach to Islam Orthodox, in
her piece, Elliott ties him very tightly to the Salafist movement—or
what she refers to as Salafiya—albeit to the "nonmilitant majority."
Salafiya, she says, has become a home to the "most conservative"
of those young American Muslims who "have grown up in a newly
hostile country, with mounting opposition to the construction of
mosques, a national movement seeking to ban courts from consult-
ing Shariah, or Islamic law, and rising hate crimes against Muslims."
Qadhi is smart, and he's devout. He relates well to young American Muslims; Elliott points out that he likes the word "dude" and

uses a "MacBook Pro (encased in Islamic apple green)." At one time he identified as a Salafi; as a rule, Elliott notes, Salafis "denounce the veneration of saints, common among some Sufi sects." In other words, with Qadhi there is not the appreciation of Sheikh Ahmad Zarruq that you find with Hamza Yusuf; nor would there be the personal identification with the saint. The theology of AlMaghrib is literalist. Before 9/11, Qadhi allowed his own criticism of Israel to devolve into attacks on Jews; in that context, he recommended a book that called the Holocaust a hoax. All of this means that nowadays he's often found himself in a difficult, though in many ways fortunate, situation, as Elliott explains:

> He is the rare Western cleric fluent in the language of militants, having spent nearly a decade studying Islam in Saudi Arabia, steeped in the same tradition that spawned Osama bin Laden's splinter movement. Arguably few American theologians are better positioned to offer an authoritative rebuttal of extremist ideology. But to do that, Qadhi says he would need to address the thorny question of what kinds of militant actions *are* permitted by Islamic law. It is a forbidden topic for most American clerics, who even refrain from criticizing their country's foreign policy for fear of being branded unpatriotic.

Within a week of the *Times* story, Qadhi had responded with a long blog post on the website *MuslimMatters*, where he is a regular contributor. In general he thought Elliott had been sympathetic to him and remarked on the ways in which he thought she'd done justice both to him and the movement he belongs to and often leads. She humanized Qadhi and made clear, he noted, that "conservative Islam is not one monolithic movement, but rather a spectrum of movements." What's more, she made the case that the extremist violence is not theological but political. Qadhi concluded his appreciation of the profile, however, with an even subtler version of the equivocation around violence that Elliott herself had addressed in the story: "In other words, the militants are not militants because Islam is an evil religion, but rather because they have strong political grievances with

America, and are then using their (mis)understanding of Islam to jus-
tify their violence." Qadhi is either so committed to the diversity of
interpretations within Islam, or perhaps sympathetic to political violence, at least as it's understood within Muslim-majority countries,
that he can't, without quibbling, suggest that terrorism is always the
unjustified result of a misunderstanding of Islam. Apparently, sometimes violent Muslims understand Islam just fine.

Qadhi's major problem with Elliott's story was her emphasis on
the concept of Salafiya itself. Because while he may agree theologi-
cally with most of what Salafis say, he no longer sees himself in those
terms, mainly because he disagrees with the way Salafis tend to deal
with "opposing groups." He goes on to say that "we in America need
to acclimatize the religious aspects of *Ahl al-Sunnah*"—believers in
the Koran and the tradition around it—"within the cultural climate
that we find ourselves in, and I go so far as to say that this is what
Islam itself intended." At the same time, taking the opportunity to
discuss Elliott's portrayal of him as the counterpoint to Anwar al-
Awlaki, the American-born al-Qaeda leader killed in Yemen by a US
drone strike in 2011, Qadhi again seems at least for a moment to pre-
varicate: "I don't view myself as being his polar opposite. I have my
message, he has his." (Although this is also, perhaps, an expression of
humility, an acknowledgment by Qadhi that he cannot possibly have
every answer to Islamic militancy around the world. To be sure, he
would want to look to Zaytuna for some help.)

Sheikh Hamza told me that Elliott had written him the morning her story appeared. She wanted to know what he thought of her
portrayal of Qadhi. (Though Hamza is not mentioned in the story,
Imam Zaid is described as taking up Qadhi's lead in condemning violent jihad: "Other American clerics have also begun to speak out,"
Elliott writes, "most notably Imam Zaid Shakir, who posted a widely
read letter online aimed at dissuading the 'would-be mujahid,' or
warrior.")

And while I cannot be sure he said as much to her directly, Sheikh
Hamza pulled no punches with me: "I think what she's showing—in
the piece—is how difficult it is to be a Muslim committed to this
premodern tradition in the modern world. And I don't think it's a

flattering picture of him. But I think the implications of what they're teaching are so much worse than what she really lets on in the article."

As I drove, I asked whether he thought Elliott understood well enough how troubling those teachings might be.

"I don't know," he replied, "she didn't go into the *al-walaa wal-baraa* anywhere near enough, and that's the key issue with them because they believe that it's disbelief to have any loyalty to a non-Muslim political entity—that you are not a Muslim."

In the story, Elliott briefly addresses the Islamic concept of *al-walaa wal-baraa*, a fringe Islamic doctrine that religion writer Reza Aslan says in his 2009 book *How to Win a Cosmic War* reflects an "uncompromising moral dichotomy" that is "not found in the Koran and totally abandoned by contemporary Islamic scholars," Hamza included. It means variously loyalty and disownment, love and hate for the sake of Allah, choosing sides in what Aslan calls a *"cosmic duality,* in which the whole of creation is partitioned into 'believers' . . . and 'unbelievers.'" Aslan here is describing the doctrine as it relates to jihadists such as al-Qaeda ideologues, but Elliott suggests that among ultraconservative Muslims in America, including Yasir Qadhi and his followers, the question of how far their love and allegiance might extend to non-Muslims remains open, even "absent the question of war." The decade-plus-long conflicts in Afghanistan and Iraq, drone strikes in Yemen and Pakistan, and other US military action in the Muslim world only raise the stakes of a question that existed before 9/11. Orthodox students of Qadhi "ponder their loyalties," she notes, while considering the lessons of the Koran. "Internet forums buzz with talk about the concept of *al-walaa wal-baraa,* which is rooted in Koranic verses dictating allegiance to Muslims over non-Muslims. Qadhi's students are divided over whether to vote, pay taxes that support the military or even celebrate Thanksgiving." On the question of citizenship, Elliott reports, Qadhi encourages his followers to vote and pay their taxes, but you won't find a student from AlMaghrib joining the US military. There Qadhi draws the line: "There is no draft. . . . Thank God for that."

"I thank God," said Hamza back in 2008, "we live in a country that at least has an understanding of due process of law. We fail to live up to the highest ideals of our legal system. But I think most Muslims in this country would prefer to be judged in an American court of law than in many courts of law in the Muslim world. And that says a lot." And it may be remarks like this that has made those Internet forums blaze against him. One reads: "There have been many other Muslim scholars who condemned the killing of the innocents in the World Trade Centre, but none crossed the limits of Al-Walaa Wal-Baraa . . . as Hamza Yusuf did."

But to be sure, a concern with appropriate Islamic allegiance and enmity had been a question at the heart of the college's mission from the start. Led by decisions Hamza made as early as the mid-'90s, the founders' answer had come together in their name—*zaytunah*, the olive, whose oil offers light without fire—and their early motto: "Where Islam Meets America." And while Yasir Qadhi is convinced that "America remains far better than any European equivalent," as he noted in a 2010 essay about why violence appeals to young Muslims, he doesn't seem to find in the nation itself what Sheikh Hamza does: a long and proud tradition of dissent and struggle toward the American ideal. And so, while America may be better for Muslims than Europe, a fact Qadhi insists "we need to appreciate and cherish," the proud struggle he's engaged in is at its heart, by his own account, an Islamic one, not an American one. And while he, like Hamza, calls America home, there seems to exist no comfortable way for Qadhi and his Orthodox Muslims to "balance our loyalties between the requirements of our faith and those that are increasingly being imposed upon us by our country." Not to put too fine a point on it, but Qadhi's Muslims are simply—perhaps even unfortunately—"in America"; Hamza's Muslims are American.

As we approached the airport, Hamza offered his final point about Yasir Qadhi and his followers. The sheikh insisted, "Really to be consistent with their teaching, they should leave; they shouldn't even be living here. You know, and I believe that. They need to go."

None of this means that Sheikh Hamza questions that Qadhi is truly a Muslim; nor does it mean Hamza believes that Qadhi, or any other Orthodox believer, is a "bad Muslim." Qadhi simply doesn't strike Sheikh Hamza as a particularly American Muslim, and for the *ummah*, whatever anxiety Qadhi inspires in his followers over this question of love and enmity represents "a real calamity and a crisis." Even the Prophet, says Hamza, loved people who were non-Muslims. With all due respect to his fellow Muslims and their differences of opinion, Hamza seems to be saying, if you don't feel any allegiance whatsoever to the country, there's just no good reason to make America home. Get out.

I'd heard Hamza in speeches make similar remarks before, that there are Muslims in America who simply don't belong here, whose legal thinking about Muslim participation in Western democracies skews so often toward *al-baraa*, or disownment, that they threaten to create "cognitive dissonance" in their followers "that leads to the type of abuse that you get with these nutcases that go off the deep end."

Even earlier that week, accepting his award from the Network of Spiritual Progressives and *Tikkun* magazine, he drew from the field of economics to describe religion's "negative externalities"—those unplanned-for social costs or "collateral damage" created when "we don't intend to harm anybody, even though we end up harming people." Corporations pollute a river and you get "babies with problems down the road." A young man is raised in Islam and attempts while aboard a plane to detonate a bomb in his underwear. Another man raised in Islam parks a car filled with explosives in the middle of Times Square and then walks away leaving a ribbon of smoke. Yet another man raised in Islam, this one an Army doctor, opens fire on a military base, killing thirteen people and wounding more than thirty others.

Yasir Qadhi lays at least some of the blame for the alienation that he believes has led to these attacks—failed or no—at the feet of religious leaders like Sheikh Hamza, though he doesn't call him out by name. And like Hamza, in that 2010 essay Qadhi points to factors he considers "external" to the individual young Muslim; when faced with what seems like mounting pressure and violence against the *ummah*— abroad and at home—and "finding nothing of significance at a local level, he then looks to more influential scholars." These are "famous national clerics and *da'ees*,"—or, Muslims who perform *dawah*, preachers or missionaries—"staple invitees to any major Islamic conference." In America, there is no invitee more staple than Hamza Yusuf. Qadhi continues: "Instead of supporting the cause of the weak and oppressed, these clerics side with the oppressors, routinely dissociating themselves from their own, giving spectacle *fatwas* against violence even as they ignore state-sponsored terrorism and what he"—the alienated young Muslim—"perceives as the 'greater violence.'"

During our conversation, Sheikh Hamza did not shy away from criticizing the government. "The state, too," he said, "they don't want to take any responsibility for the madness that they've created. This whole way of dealing with problems—what they've done in Iraq and Afghanistan, or the Israeli thing—it's all this failure of these political leaders that generates so much—" He hesitated. Once again, the idea he seemed to be searching for was "trouble." This problem with the state has been a common theme, as well: in his discussion with Blankinship, where he proposed that the sacred responsibility of the American Muslim is dissent in the model of Thoreau; on his blog, where in February, as Egyptians rose in revolt against Hosni Mubarak, he'd written, "America, where are you?"; in the White House, where he advised President Bush against the wars that would consume the nation for more than a decade to follow; and in any number of public talks on the place of Islam in the West, where he'd argued that the greatest martyr is the one who speaks against unjust authority and dies for it. "That," he's said, "should be the voice of Islam in this country."

In his mind, that's the American Muslim citizen they're training at Zaytuna. Writing in their 2008 book *Agenda to Change Our Condition*, Sheikh Hamza and Imam Zaid foresee Muslims, through small, grassroots organizing and the establishment of new and productive institutions like their own, playing a leading role in the "direct citizen involvement in local politics." These Muslims will be part of "the reinventing of American democracy."[1] When fueled by the right balance of social capital, and intellectual and financial capital—terms Zaid and

---

[1] In *Agenda to Change Our Condition*, Imam Zaid and Shaykh Hamza rely on Carmen Sirianni and Lewis Friedland's 2001 book *Civic Innovation in America: Community Empowerment, Public Policy, and the Movement for Civic Renewal*. It is here that Sirianni and Friedland originally make the point about the "reinventing of American democracy."

Hamza rely on in their *Agenda*, written in anticipation of the college— American Muslims can emerge with new possibilities for civic life. "If we could constructively bring these two reservoirs of capital together, we could develop a model that could initiate a revolution in American civic participation. That revolution lies in our potential to reverse one of the most damaging implications of suburban sprawl—the depletion of intellectual and material resources from the inner-city." Of this approach to being an American Muslim, Brooklyn's Imam Siraj Wahhaj has perhaps said it best: "Islam came to deal with the inequalities in the neighborhood." And at Zaytuna if these issues are not yet on a course syllabus, they're most definitely on the agenda.

In this regard, Zaytuna is moving American Muslims in what's typically seen as a progressive direction, one that would be virtually impossible without an Islamic groundwork that supports engagement in our national civic and economic life. How else to engage with the quintessential American problems of suburban sprawl and inequality but to embrace politics and "worldly matters" as "part of an effort to improve the world we live in"?

But on that point about progressiveness, Hamza would want to make it clear that he's not exactly the man that Rabbi Lerner and *Tikkun* magazine think he is. He's been outspoken on the need for American Muslims to engage civically and behave socially in ways that are usually considered politically conservative. Writing on his blog in November 2010 about how Muslims should respond to outbreaks of anti-Islamic sentiment around the country—to say nothing of America's ongoing foreign wars—he reminded his readers that while the American Left, "despite its moral ambiguity on many such personal and social issues, has a far better track record of standing firmly against warmongering, arms proliferation, and American aggression in countries where we don't belong[,] . . . there is also a progressive Right that we forget about best embodied in Ron Paul, who is one of the most outspoken critics of warmongering and American foreign wars and misadventures." What's more, American "conservatives are as troubled as Muslims are about the predominance of premarital and extramarital sexuality, the breakdown of the family, and the proliferation of pornography and drugs."

And as we pulled into the Emirates terminal at San Francisco International Airport, the conversation had already shifted from what liberal arts courses Hamza would most likely teach at Zaytuna—in the near term, poetry and astronomy—to what he called "the problem of the modern genius." He'd been thinking about it since he'd picked up Hubert Dreyfus and Sean Dorrance Kelly's *All Things Shining: Reading the Western Classics to Find Meaning in a Secular Age*, part of his ongoing education in the tradition of the great books. Bob Dylan, he said, really understood what's at the heart of genius, an appreciation that what beauty comes from you doesn't originate in you. "And if you watch in all those interviews," Hamza said, "he would always say that. When he was praised he would put his head down. Because he knew the power of the muse. There's too much mystery." And then he misquoted a line from the *Odyssey*.

Maashaa Allah.

But as we began unpacking the car and piled the family's luggage on the curb, Sheikh Hamza once again changed course. He seemed concerned that in all our conversation I might have gotten the wrong impression of him.

"I think it's funny, Lerner giving me that prize. I'm not really a spiritual progressive," he said. "I draw lines."

And whether he's aware of it or not, if Zaytuna is to become a liberal arts college, in the model of religious institutions like Georgetown, Marquette, or Brandeis—or Harvard, Princeton, and Yale, for that matter—it will have to at least address some of these lines, and probably cross them eventually. If Zaytuna is to continue impressing its students with a diverse and relevant American community, it will have to at least ask whether an American liberal arts college can succeed if it's founded on primarily conservative principles. (Conservative Christian colleges often find themselves asking the very same thing.) At the moment, on one point certainly, Hamza's not budging.

"I don't want to see gay people bashed," he said just before we parted, as he prepared for the regular TSA routine for men with names like Hamza Yusuf. "But I also don't want it normalized as a healthy thing for a society. I think it confuses young people who are already having enough things to deal with.

"Neuroplasticity has shown us that sexual identity is fluid," he continued, and he found himself on a roll. "You can actually become a homosexual very easily. . . . The brain refigures itself. I mean that's one of the things they found about pornography. [One scientist] was arguing that people that actually view a lot of pornography start having homoerotic tendencies, because they're being aroused with male images. And so the brain actually begins to rewire."

The question about whether Zaytuna would welcome an openly gay or lesbian student had come up earlier in the year; a caller to Michael Krasny's San Francisco public radio program *Forum* had raised the issue during Imam Zaid and Sheikh Hamza's appearance in September.

Would someone like that be allowed?

Sheikh Hamza answered flatly. "I don't know why they want to attend a school—" He stopped himself. He seemed to want to complete the thought with "like Zaytuna."

"I don't want things normalized," he said to me at the departures terminal. The car was now completely emptied of bags. We were just standing there. "I don't want someone to say this is a normal, healthy lifestyle. It's not. It's pathogenic. Lesbianism is a little more problematic. But male-on-male is pathogenic. I worked with a gastroenterologist." Hamza had a nursing degree.

"I saw it, I saw it," he went on. "I saw the effects of rectal intercourse. Even now that they've done it in the heterosexual community. That's all from pornography. It's not a natural thing. It leads to infection. For me, those things, I have lines that I'm not going to cross over to be politically correct.

"But on the other hand," he concluded, "I don't want to see this horrible, intolerant world."

And he mentioned he had family members who are gay.

In September he had said he didn't know, but there is an answer to Sheikh Hamza's question about why an LGBT Muslim might someday want to come to a school like Zaytuna. Indeed, someday soon, if there's not one there in the closet already. It's largely the same reason Zaytuna Institute was so popular and why the students at the college have never been late to one of his classes. It's why thousands gather to hear him speak and why there are probably thousands more who decided to become Muslims in the first place.

Hamza Yusuf is the reason—along with Imam Zaid—why anyone right now would want to attend Zaytuna College. This is what their students have told me. And across the country, gay or straight—and I say this because some of those followers simply must be gay—Muslims love these men for their sacred knowledge and their agenda to change the condition of Muslims in this country. And yet, if Zaid and Hamza and Hatem have their way, it won't always be like this. One day, Zaytuna College itself, the institution and the students it's preparing for Muslim American citizenship, will be the draw. As it stands, that's the only hope for a gay or lesbian Muslim who applies and is accepted to the college. The classes will grow. And God willing, the students themselves will have to make the institution more welcoming and more diverse, reflective of American society at large. In this case they'll have to change their own condition and offer the most sophisticated answer to the question of gay Muslims. They may have to put into practice a lesson Hamza himself taught over four hours that day at Cooper Union. In standing for the truth, Zaytunies may at some point have to cross the line and stand against the Muslim who introduced the truth to them in the first place.

ELEVEN

Jesus, the Son of Mary
(Peace Be upon Them)

> On the authority of 'Abd Allah bin 'Amir—The messenger
> of God said, "Jesus, the Son of Mary, will descend to the
> earth, marry, have children, and remain for forty-five years.
> After that, he will die and be buried next to my grave. Then
> Jesus, the Son of Mary, and I shall arise from one grave be-
> tween Abu Bakr and 'Umar."
>
> —Ibn al-Jawzi

For April 22, Good Friday evening in the Christian world, Dustin
and several of the women from the school were organizing a small
mawlid in the Zaytuna library, inviting a few of their friends from
the Bay Area to join in honoring the birth of the Prophet with some
poetry and prayer, recitation, tea, and light snacks. Though he'd officially left the school, Dustin would bring incense to burn.

I'd been invited when I met a few of the sisters for coffee during a
break in the proceedings of a conference I'd been attending for much
of the day. Organized by Dr. Hatem and hosted by the UC Berkeley
Center for Race and Gender, the two-day event was called "Islamophobia Production and Re-Defining the Global 'Security' Agenda
for the 21st Century." Munir Jiwa had given a talk about how the
media shapes the debate around Islam; the "Five 'Media Pillars' of
Islam," he said, begin with 9/11, highlight jihad and terrorism, focus
on whether women wear veils, raise questions about Islam's compat-
ibility with the West, and ultimately make a narrow case about Islam
in the Middle East by mainly covering the conflict between Israel
and Palestine. Sister Marianne Farina had moderated a panel about
the relationship between Islam and what the organizers had called
the "Security State." Plans by American law enforcement to map

Muslim communities was compared by civil rights attorney Veena Dubal, who was currently representing six clients on the TSA no-fly list, to what "Hitler did when leading up to gathering and killing Jews." The conference had mainly been designed to build a network of academics—the Islamophobia Study Circle, Hatem called it—that could research the kinds of networks ginning up fear of Muslims in the United States. By the end of the day, when Hatem, who identifies as much as an activist as a scholar, offered his academic philosophy—"research must have a direct impact on the community"—I wasn't sure how closely they'd hewed to the theory.

The panels covered much of the same ground as a class Hatem was teaching at Berkeley that he called simply Islamophobia. I'd been sitting in when I could. Speaking one day about the congressional hearings on American Muslim radicalization, Hatem essentially called New York representative Peter King, the organizer of the hearings, a modern-day cross between Pontius Pilate and Joseph McCarthy. "If Jesus was here," Hatem said, "he'd be arrested as a Communist!"

The student Jamye Ford was taking this class in addition to his full course load at Zaytuna. Sumaya and Rasheeda would also occasionally show up, but Jamye seemed fully committed. The women had let on as much when I'd spoken with them in February. They'd referred to Jamye as mini-Superman, second only to Imam Zaid. Like with Zaid, whom Faatimah had once referred to as "the best student in his own class," the Muslim superpower was not strength or agility or magic; it was productivity. Zaid and Hamza's *Agenda to Change Our Condition* reminded their followers that "modern life is a concerted conspiracy to deprive us of our precious time."

After waiting for more than an hour in the Zaytuna lounge for Dustin and a few others to arrive, including a local white convert emcee and poet known as Baraka Blue and another friend named Haroon, who would lead the Arabic prayers and songs, we circled up on the rugs covering the floors of the library. The prayer was mainly sung in a call and response. The melodies were mainly familiar to me now; I'd picked them up the same way I'd picked up my Catholic hymns as a child, through repetition. These were the prayers of the mawlid at Ta'leef Collective and the grand celebration in Santa Clara in February.

I'd come, by this point, to understand that time spent in regular mawlid celebration was not uncommon among the Zaytunies or their families at home, but also that mawlids are not universally loved in the *ummah*. Over the centuries there has been no little controversy over whether it is okay to mark the birth of the Prophet by gathering to eat, sing, dance, and pray in his honor. Whole books have been written on the topic, and these, the earliest of which dates back to the eleventh century, like other legal rulings (or fatwas) that concern the behavior of the Muslims, measure the practice on a scale from "compulsory," "meritorious," and "permissible," to "reprehensible" and ultimately "forbidden." Even things as seemingly insignificant as the order in which someone removes his shoes upon entering the mosque—right first or left first, which also applies when considering the foot he leads with when stepping into or out of the toilet—gets measured along this scale, though not in either extreme. (At the mosque, it's better to remove the left shoe first, then the right, a pattern you reverse on your way out; and as for the toilet, lead with the left on the way in and the right on the way out. In time, of course, patterns like these become second nature; you do them by force of habit.)

Some deeply conservative Muslims believe gatherings like the one this night—to say nothing of the Grand Mawlid headlined by Sheikh Hamza—are absolutely reprehensible, as with other forms of religious innovation. Entered into with "total abandon," they become prohibited. There are also those who would prohibit the mawlid out of hand: How, they ask, could any practice be considered good if it wasn't known and practiced by the Prophet himself? To claims made by some Muslims who believe the Prophet himself visits the mawlids, the blind sheikh Abdul Aziz ibn Baz, a twentieth-century Saudi Arabian scholar of great renown and great controversy—the grand mufti, for whom the office itself was revived, and who was called upon by Osama bin Laden to resign his post after endorsing with a fatwa the Middle East peace process—wrote on the matter: "This is the greatest falsehood and worst form of ignorance because the Prophet shall never come out of his grave before the Day of Resurrection."

These students at Zaytuna were learning something different, however: a lesson in Islamic creativity that began with their first assignment of the year—Dr. Umar's essay on *bid'a* and *ijtihad*. While they all seemed to acknowledge and respect the diversity of opinion on innovation such as this, in their eyes, the whole point seemed to be to celebrate the life of Muhammad—and what could be wrong with that? And since the teachers around here all reveled in the mawlid, here we were. (Imam Zaid is also known to fast on Mondays, the day of the week the Prophet is said to have been born; one Monday evening in March, he broke fast in the middle of a conversation we were having over the phone and had to apologize more than once for talking with his mouth full.)

After the Arabic, Baraka Blue recited his own poem about the Prophet, which was met with the kind of verbal appreciation you expect following a good meal. They sang more, led mainly by Sumaya. There was silence. And they laughed, too. In the end, said Baraka Blue, they were there "to establish the mawlid in Berkeley forever. . . . We begin it now; may it never end. May it be written among those who strove to establish it. For generations to come, may it be written among those who strove to establish it. And may it be as well established in our hearts." This was a Friday night with the students at Zaytuna, and it was meant to be like this forever.

Rasheeda prepared to read her own poem.

"You ready?" said Baraka Blue.

"Yes," she replied.

Bismillah.

Whereas Baraka Blue had written about the Prophet, Rasheeda's poem was addressed to Khadija: "all you could do was marry him."

When Rasheeda finished the poem, Mahassin said, "Read it again."

When she finished a second time, under his breath Dustin said, "Oh, man . . ." Then she read just a few more.

As I sat looking on as these men and women bowed their heads and as I listened to their poetry, the mawlids—grand and small—struck me as expressions of joy. The songs were announcements of delight in support of the stories they told of the Prophet. And yet, when remembering the Prophet, there were moments when the Zaytunies—starting, of course, with Sheikh Hamza—could grow so invested in the story and in the Prophet's memory that they found themselves in tears. Of the students, Sumaya seemed more affected than anyone else. The mawlids were so emotional for her that they seemed to bring together the heights of joy and the darkest, most fragile and vulnerable parts of her prayer life. The parts she needs God for. Leading the songs this evening, Sumaya would sometimes have to pause to collect herself. When it happened the first time I'd assumed she'd lost the words; when it happened again, I realized the Prophet had overwhelmed her.

I left the library not long after Rasheeda finished reading her poems. Dustin led everyone in what I'd thought was a closing prayer on behalf of a Native American community trying to reclaim land the city had long ago developed into a parking lot. On my way back to where I was staying in Oakland, I received a text message from Mahassin: "Leenah is upset that you left, so am I for that matter. The night is young!!! I should have made an effort in persuading you to stay. What's the off chance that I can get you to come back."

I couldn't return tonight, I told her: "I'm sorry! Let's get together again tomorrow," I wrote. "Will you all forgive me?"

I was on my way to meet a friend for a drink.

"No! Lol, just joking. Of course! See you tomorrow insha-Allah."

Allah didn't will that we'd see each other the next day, but in the late afternoon, Leenah sent me a series of text messages:

> 5:25: Hey Scott, are you doing anything for Easter Sunday tomorrow? We kinda wanna tag along, if that's cool?
>
> 5:53: But we'd totally understand if you wish to spend the day alone.
>
> 5:53: No pressure, ever:)

Easter with the Zaytunies. If the mawlid was considered by some to be a prohibited innovation, what would Allah say about this?

I let Leenah know I thought it was a great idea. I quickly found a Catholic Church in Berkeley where we could go. "In terms of clothing," she asked, "anything in particular that we should wear (i.e., skirts instead of pants)?" I thumbed a reply:

6:37: However you're comfortable. How you all normally dress is perfect. We can get breakfast after too. Traditional Easter morning thing.

Zaytuna's relationship with Jesus goes back further than Leenah and Sumaya, Rasheeda and Faatimah and Mahassin and me, of course. It's important to remember that the origin story about the yurt in Hayward involves a Catholic nun advising the former Christian Sheikh Hamza that American Muslims ought to have a college to call their own. Hamza had done a translation of the sayings of Jesus based on traditional Arabic sources.

According to al-Hadram—Once someone asked Jesus, "How are you able to walk on water?"
    Jesus replied, "With certainty."
    Then someone said, "But we also have certainty!"
    Jesus then asked them, "Are stone, clay, and gold equal in your eyes?"
    They replied, "Certainly not!"
    Jesus responded, "They are in mine."

And when they needed a place to hold classes, Christians had been the ones to rent them rooms. According to Paul Martin, president of the American Baptist Seminary of the West, one of the nine religious schools that make up the Graduate Theological Union, the agreement came together over the course of many months. During the economic downturn, the seminary Martin leads lost some tenants from UC Berkeley, which had been renting some 85 percent of the school. This opened up the sixteen hundred square feet that Zaytuna would make its home.

From Martin's perspective, "This was like a gift from God." He had never heard of Zaytuna before his seminary's rental agency brought them the possibility of sharing space. And presented with the prospect of opening the seminary to a new college, Martin described going through a process of "due diligence," concerned first of all that ABSW's faculty and staff would be okay with a Muslim school moving in. "For me," he said, "it would have been a problem if there had been some outcry." But from the faculty and staff there was no resistance whatsoever. And though he'd worried that a couple of conservative board members might have some reservations, they likewise raised no concern. When I spoke with Martin in November, the school hadn't yet been able to systematically assess the reaction of the student body, but there hadn't really been a chance for the Muslims and the Baptists to interact. Zaytuna used a separate entrance and held their classes during the day; the American Baptist Seminary was a night school. Martin assured me, though, that his students were aware Zaytuna had moved in. And there had been no complaints— not from the community, at least.

Some of the strongest support for their decision to open the seminary to Zaytuna had come from the dean of the Graduate Theological Union, which Martin explained was one of only two or three communities of its kind in the country. No other was so closely affiliated with a liberal arts university with the stature of UC Berkeley. Beginning a relationship with Zaytuna very quickly came to be seen as a way for the Baptists specifically, and the GTU more generally, to realize, he said, "a vision we have for interfaith dialogue." They'd already had preliminary discussions with Omar Nawaz about sharing faculty someday, hosting events together, and opening up ways for students to cross-register. Once Zaytuna is accredited, Martin said, they would begin following through with that last possibility. "As much as you can dream for this," he said, "it just blows my mind as a seminary administrator of the potential right here at our doorstep. All we've got to do is walk across campus."

Martin's due diligence involved, in part, looking over the media coverage of Zaytuna, including Fox News's original "Educate or

Indoctrinate?" report from 2009 and other coverage from CNN. And when presenting the school's need for space, Omar had warned the school's Administrative Cabinet, Martin said, about the attention and scrutiny anyone affiliated with Muslim institutions can draw. Like Barbara Bradley Hagerty's NPR story on the opening of Zaytuna, the Associated Press report by Terence Chea had run nationally on September 9; both made mention of the seminary. The AP report on the opening of the school gave space to Frank Gaffney, who suggested that Zaytuna was "promoting in the United States incubators for Shariah"—the "stealth jihad." (No one at Zaytuna would deny teaching the shariah; they just don't see it as "jihad"—stealth or otherwise.) The AP's Chea referred specifically in his report to the American Baptist Seminary of the West; Hagerty was less precise, noting simply that Zaytuna's students had "settled themselves in a classroom rented from an American Baptist seminary building." And immediately, Martin said, "once this information got out—that a Baptist seminary is providing space for an Islamic college—the emails started bouncing off the walls." Messages were "coming from everyplace," from people they didn't even know. "Just a whole lot of stuff!" he said, his voice rising.

Martin told me that after the story had made it to CNN, a network that didn't mention the seminary in its report, he'd heard from one woman who complained, "We just can't believe that a Baptist seminary would provide space for an Islamic terrorist organization." Not everyone had the same message, of course. Still, that woman provided the tenor for nearly half of the email he received, and those, he said, "tend to stand out." When I asked whether there was any local response from the Berkeley community or local media, Martin said no. "You're the first person I've talked to."

When the deal was finally closed on a five-year lease with an extension for another five—at a reported annual cost of $230,000—Martin and the seminary pushed very hard to complete renovations Zaytuna had in mind for offices, designated classroom space, a prayer room, and the library. They also upgraded a small kitchen. Whether all this would be accomplished in time for the opening of the school seemed to have been partly to blame for the early mystery about where Zaytuna College would open its doors. And, Martin said, there was also the "issue of the homeless that sleep on the curbs." As Sheikh Hamza had pointed out on Michael Krasny's radio program *Forum* back in September, Zaytuna had opened across the street from People's Park, daytime home of much of Berkeley's homeless population. In the evenings, when the park closes to the public, they scatter to the curbs in the neighborhood, and, said Martin, "they do all their business on property." The back entryway to the seminary building provided exceptionally good cover, and while in previous years that entrance hadn't been much used, with Zaytuna moving in, it would essentially become the front door to the college.

Martin, Omar, and the seminary's head of facilities had all met with the people who would retreat to this place in the evenings. The Baptists had seen it as a kind of outreach in the Christian model he'd preached from the Gospel of Matthew: "Whatever you did for one of the least of these brothers and sisters of mine, you did for me." Martin had told them, "You can sleep here, but by 7 a.m. you have to move on." And since the school had been open he'd been making regular rounds. They'd virtually disappeared.

A native of Los Angeles who studied theology in Virginia, Paul Martin's introduction to Islam came in the '60s, when he worked as an associate of Martin Luther King Jr. as part of the civil rights movement. "First it was the Black Muslims," he told me, "which we got up with. We had a good relationship with them over the years, and did not see them in the same way as other people saw them. We have to work together. We applauded them for their work with black males." But the Muslims were not committed to nonviolence. And with King, "you had to be taught to be nonviolent." Martin confessed, though: "I never did learn. . . . They used to call me 'California,' because I came from California to go to seminary. And Martin used to say, 'Now everybody be in the front except 'California'—put him in the back.'"

He told me a story of driving King from the airport to the Second Baptist Church in Los Angeles, which had become a formative congregation for the civil rights leader, the first and last in Los Angeles to host him. On this particular day, with Second Baptist filled to capacity, a young Paul Martin would sit behind Martin Luther King and Malcolm X, "a brilliant man," he said. "I heard them talk." About what exactly he couldn't recall. "They sat there and they talked. The press never put that out. . . . He was very supportive of Martin that Sunday afternoon."

It was ultimately Paul Martin's own history in support of Martin Luther King that brought us to our final words about Zaytuna. I wanted to know whether "California" saw any similarity between his own struggle with King and what American Muslims were facing today. Were those emails filled with the same bile that, in the '60s, had led old ladies to spit on him or men to drop bags of urine onto black protesters below? These experiences he had known. And based on that, he had his guess about what it was to be a Muslim: "African Americans don't want to take over America; they just want a part of the pie. I don't think Muslim Americans want to take over America. They want to be accepted like we want to be accepted—as full citizens and participants in the life of America. And those doors have historically been shut for all of us. And are still being shut."

And yet, there was a major difference, he said. "I did not see a fear factor as much in the civil rights movement." This sort of fear—of life and limb—was new to America. "It's different from what we experienced." And that fear was something Martin himself felt. "We all suffer under that—whether we buy into it or not." The events of 9/11 were mainly to blame: "Even I sat there amazed," he said. The world had been absolutely bewildered.

And what about all those American blacks marching with and behind King?

"We," Martin told me, "we did not cast that kind of fear." And he surprised me with what he said next, about his due diligence. The media highlights the extremism; that we know. And for Martin this seemed "rightfully so, so that we understand that they can create chaos."

I could only assume he'd meant the extremists.

He then told me he didn't see the nation getting over our fear in this lifetime. He paused for a moment, a man of Martin Luther King's generation who'd seen Barack Obama elected.

"Mine or yours."

· · ·

As had become typical, it was Rasheeda, Mahassin and Leenah, Faatimah and Sumaya—a nearly inseparable bunch—who arrived to meet me at the Downtown Berkeley BART station. On the walk to the church Faatimah told me about spending time with Dustin the day before, protesting with the Native American community he'd prayed for Friday night. Like academic work, it seemed, prayer was best when it involved a direct impact on the community.

For months I'd been led through mosques and community centers, lining up shoulder-to-shoulder for prayer and making room on the sidewalk when the masjid was filled to capacity. I'd been instructed in the best way to remove my shoes and how properly to fold my hands. Prayer in the Muslim world was something you had to learn. And once you learned it, prayer was something you never forgot. It became second nature, which was part of its purpose. Imam Zaid had instructed his students how to pray with their every breath.

I hadn't been to Easter Mass for a number of years, but the notion that prayer was unforgettable applied here as well. When we arrived for 9:30 Mass at Saint Joseph the Worker Church, the women filed in behind me as I brought them up along the side aisle to a pew about midway through the sanctuary. The first thing Faatimah noticed was that where Mary appeared in the church statuary she was in a hijab.

Before joining them in our pew, I situated myself briefly in the bench in front of them and explained what would happen during the service. There would be standing and sitting and kneeling. There would be readings about the Resurrection, something Muslims don't believe had happened to Jesus or was even possible yet. "We are witnesses to all that he did both in Judea and in Jerusalem," we would hear. "They put him to death by hanging him on a tree; but God raised him on the third day and allowed him to appear, not to all the people but to us who were chosen by God as witnesses, and who ate and drank with him after he rose from the dead. He commanded us to preach to the people and to testify that he is the one ordained by God as judge of the living and the dead. All the prophets testify about him that everyone who believes in him receives forgiveness of sins through his name" (Acts 10:39–43).

In Islam, Jesus was one of the six great prophets, and the one who most recently preceded Muhammad. The others include Adam, Noah, Abraham, and Moses. Leenah would explain that, as she understood it, the difference between these prophets and the countless others in the history of Islam was that the great six would face the most intense tribulation.

In the surah of the Koran named for his mother Mary, Jesus speaks miraculously from the cradle: "Blessed was I on the day I was born, and blessed shall I be on the day of my death and on the day I shall be raised to life" (Koran 19:33–34). None of this had yet come to pass, though; Jesus had not died, but had been raised up by Allah body and soul. It was widely believed that before the Crucifixion, one of the disciples was made to look like Jesus and was killed in his place. Jesus went up through a hole in the roof of the house. (Another verse in the Koran says about the Jews supposed to have killed Jesus, "They declared: 'We have put to death the Messiah, Jesus the son of Mary, the apostle of God.' They did not kill him, nor did they crucify him but they thought they did" [Koran 4:157]. This notion that these Jews "thought they did" kill Jesus can be literally translated, "he was made to resemble another for them.") This was the version Leenah had once told me, and there was a day still to come when Jesus would return.

The women didn't draw particular attention from the congregation, it seemed to me. I'd warned them before the service began that at a certain point I'd get up with everyone else and walk to the front of the church to receive Communion. They should stay behind. (Many Catholics might have said the same thing about me, an unmarried man with a child on the way, who also wasn't a regular churchgoer.) I also warned them that just before Communion everyone in the church would make a sign of peace; I compared it with Islam's salaams. Some people would probably hug, but mainly they'd just offer to shake hands. Bearing in mind that these women typically avoided physical contact with men, today I advised them to do whatever they were most comfortable with. Hamza and Zaid had written that there are certain situations where not shaking hands might be insulting: "This is a problem even some of the great scholars of this time grapple with."

When the service was over I found the priest near the altar and introduced the women. I explained that they'd asked to see what Easter service was like, that they'd had an interest in Jesus. He seemed pleased to meet them and reached out to shake all their hands. They all thanked him and we made our way on to the breakfast I'd promised. We found a table at a restaurant in downtown Berkeley called Cyprus; they served Mediterranean and Persian cuisine and advertised an American breakfast, which is what we'd all order.

"That was my first time," Leenah said.

"That's what it's like," I replied.

In fact, none of them had ever been to a Christian service before. And truth be told, I said, I hadn't been particularly impressed by the Easter Mass. I'd hoped for more, especially since the Christians were celebrating the most important day of the calendar. I found myself apologizing for the priest, who'd said very little that could be considered inspiring in his homily. They didn't seem to have noticed, but mainly he'd offered a retelling of the Resurrection itself, a story Christians know as well as they know anything. It's true, I said, "he did a little with metaphor of the sun and darkness: 'Most people go into the season in the dark, just like Mary did, but then their eyes have to be opened to the Resurrection.'" I agreed that this was the right message, and it was the truth of the day itself—Easter is about seeing the world through the light and promise of new life. But I told them that when I go to Mass I want to sense that the priest is at least trying to make a connection between what's going on inside his church and what's happening in the world that awaits us outside. There was nothing like this here.

My experience of the imams at the Lighthouse Mosque, however, had been quite different. Perhaps it's easier to see what's going on in the world when the masjid actually overflows onto the sidewalk. "That's why I'm in love with the Bay!" Leenah said, and the other sisters agreed. This same sense of connection wasn't, however, what they knew from their communities around the country.

"Although it is supposed to be," Sumaya said. This was what they were learning in their jurisprudence class. "The Friday sermon is supposed to inspire people; it's supposed to be something you take with you into the rest of the week, that you apply to your life."

I'd already forgotten nearly everything the priest had said.

For the next two hours the women peppered me with questions about the Church. I found myself defining words such as "parish"—a church community—and "altar"—that area at the top where the priest stands. Sumaya asked what we'd all done when we filed out of the pews during Communion. I explained the practice going back to Jesus's Last Supper and that Catholics and Protestants disagreed over whether the bread we received from the priest had literally become the body of Christ.

After this, Sumaya asked, "So, do they eat it?"

I explained the significance of the standing and the sitting and the kneeling. You kneel before the body of Christ. You stand when the priest comes and goes. They were all various signs of reverence and respect given what was happening during the service. "Kind of like when we stand," Leenah added.

We talked about how the Gospels present Christians with essentially the same story in four slightly different versions; I emphasized the poetry of John's Gospel and the bare-bones Greek language of Mark. How Jesus's genealogy in Matthew goes back to Abraham and through King David, whom Sumaya reminded us was a prophet in Islam, whereas in Luke, Jesus's line goes all the way back to Adam. Mark had no genealogy at all; John takes Jesus, the Word, back to the creation of everything. These differences, I said, hadn't "seemed to upset the belief system of Christians." The four Gospels the women compared with their four *madhhabs.*

I explained the difference between the Old and New Testaments —"only Christians would call the Old Testament the Old Testament; for Jews it was the only testament." When Mahassin asked where the Psalms come in, I explained that no, they hadn't come from Jesus; tradition says they come from the prophet David. But, I said, you might hear echoes from the Psalms in what Jesus preached because as a Jew he would have been familiar with them. It was a little, I continued, like when you hear the language and wisdom of the Koran in what Sheikh Hamza teaches.

When I asked if they knew John the Baptist, Leenah told me that his tomb is in Damascus.

They all wondered why it was that Christian saints weren't recognized as such until they had died. I explained that sainthood indicates a special place in the afterlife, a recognition of your place with God. In Islam, as I'd learned in the case of Ahmad Zarruq, sainthood was achievable in this life—although it wasn't at all clear it was something to pursue. Leenah explained that the title "saint" is synonymous with "friend of God," and loving God was the ultimate goal in life. In fact, it wasn't that Muslims pursue sainthood; what the Muslim pursues is closeness with Allah, and in that individuals are seen by other saints as being saints themselves. Habib Umar bin Hafiz had recently visited the Bay; a descendant of the Prophet himself, with sainthood stretching back in his family generation after generation, now here was a saint, they all agreed. And so, they said, was Hamza. Zaid too. The men might all deny it—which was itself a part of sainthood—but the beloved scholars these women had encountered this year were true "friends of God." Before he left to return to Yemen, Umar bin Hafiz asked his followers to pray for him, a request that perplexed and humbled the women.

It turned out that Sumaya's favorite part of Mass had been the sign of peace, which reminded her of some of their gatherings at the masjid. When it came time to shake hands with the Christians all around them, not one of them hesitated. "I kind of wish we could have said hello to everybody."

TWELVE

Year One

The angelic realm has been eliminated from the human
condition. People don't believe in angels anymore. But I
can guarantee you, if Allah wished, he could remove the veil
right now and you would be bewildered by what you see.
                                                —Hamza Yusuf

For big fund-raising events like the one I attended in New Brunswick, New Jersey, near the end of May, both Imam Zaid and Sheikh
Hamza have handlers who escort them through rooms of their ad-
mirers. Though Zaid often arrives at the Lighthouse Mosque in
Oakland unaccompanied, and on his way to deliver the sermon has
to step over and around congregants seated on the floor, reaching
down to shake hands or affectionately squeeze someone's shoulder, at
fund-raising events he, like Sheikh Hamza, is typically accompanied
by men slightly more robust or youthful than himself. Given the mild
wilting effect this year had had on both of them, a good man certainly
wouldn't have been hard to find.

As handlers will, these men do their best to move Hamza and
Zaid on their way once they've spent adequate time with any given
person or small group, or they run interference whenever either
scholar seems to require it. And these two founding Zaytunies work
the room somewhat differently, with Zaid more inclined to flit
about from table to table, often revealing his wingspan and offering
a sweeping embrace, and Hamza a little more reserved, especially
today, walking with a cane following a fall in his office, after a while
simply waiting for guests to come to him. Here is the sign of real
charisma: You can work a room without getting up from your seat.

At some point during fund-raising events like this, a line typically forms near where Hamza sits, almost always at a table front and

center near the stage. Hamza greets his followers warmly, but also with the look of someone who knows he should remember a name but doesn't. Often there's someone seated at the side of the stage, as well, his eyes trained on Hamza; he always looks comfortable and casual, legs crossed and leaning back, but you have to assume this person is positioned to step in should any trouble arise. I've more than once been asked by this person to step aside, to take my seat or clear the way. In these cases, Hamza had either had enough or was about to take the stage. But you must assume that he's faced threats over the years—from both within and without the Muslim world—given his public opinions calling out Muslims who don't claim any allegiance to the country and addressing those non-Muslims who assume any statement he makes concerning real, democratic civic engagement is all part of an elaborate ruse, a "stealth jihad."

Zaid signs autographs on the inside covers of Zaytuna catalogs, and both Zaid and Hamza pose for group photos. They are undoubtedly priming the pump. Fund-raising is the purpose of the day.

Hamza was ushered into the ballroom while it was still empty almost an hour earlier; he brought me with him and ordered a tea and some aspirin. He'd hurt his head during that fall in his office, and even sustained a little whiplash, he said. "I don't know what happened. It all happened so fast." He hadn't been perfectly well since his *umrah* trip to Saudi Arabia, where he'd come down with something awful. Perhaps it really was too bad he'd left his sweater behind in the car that afternoon at the airport.

As usual he'd been reading a lot, including a new book called *The Convert*, which he'd been sent by the author, biographer Deborah Baker. He hadn't thought when the book had arrived that he'd have much time for it, but Baker's take on the life of the Jewish-born Muslim convert Maryam Jameelah completely won him over. "It was an incredible read," he told me. Attracted to the teachings of Pakistani fundamentalist and militant Islamist Abul Ala Maududi, as his disciple Jameelah became a writer of pamphlets and books that, Hamza said, he and Zaid both read when they converted to Islam. Her influence in the Muslim world is undeniable, Baker would argue, in large part because her sharp, often bitter manifestoes relate the story of a Jewish girl from the suburbs of New York City who abandoned the comfort and relative luxury of the United States to live in Pakistan as a convert to Islam. She represented something for the American convert to aspire to, which by American standards didn't sound particularly aspirational. Her anti-materialism, though, was exactly the point. Once settled in the household of her mentor, she wrote to tell her parents what it was like. Baker quotes Jameelah in *The Convert*: "The house itself is somewhat dingy and primitive, at least by the materialist standards of Americans, but is well built of stone and cement. A Westinghouse fridge sits in the dining room but the two bathrooms consist of nothing more than chamber pots and a cold-water shower with an unreliable pump. As there are no closets, no one knew what to do with my hangers. . . . At night we sleep in rope beds and on the hottest nights the servants carry these beds to the roof. To escape the mosquitoes, everyone pulls their covers over their heads, giving the roof the appearance of being littered with corpses." (Jameelah's public writing and her private correspondence offered vastly different accounts, which means that details like these didn't necessarily make it into her books.) Within that first year she'd publish *Islam versus the West*, her first book, released in 1962.

Hamza's assessment of Jameelah: "She's completely mad." And this was not just his opinion. Within a year of arriving in Pakistan, Jameelah had for a time been committed to a psychiatric hospital. (Jameelah died October 31, 2012. She was seventy-eight.)

Hamza had also read, on the plane to the East Coast, anthropologist Janine Wedel's book *Shadow Elite*, about the privatization of government and the profiteering of those she calls "flexians"—self-serving and slippery functionaries who move easily and often between public and private life. Hamza mentioned Dick Cheney; Wedel highlights Robert Rubin and Larry Summers. And though he loved the book— "Once in a while you get these amazing synthesizers"—he found Wedel's coinage a little silly. "People like to coin words," he said. Although Malcolm Gladwell had done well with *The Tipping Point* and *Outliers*, he thought, nowadays "all these guys aspire to something like that—a Shakespearean impact on the English language."

Thomas Friedman's *The World Is Flat*? "So stupid. Please stop." Hamza also hates portmanteaus.

What had appealed about Wedel's book, beyond its bringing together so much of what he'd been reading about the financial crisis
and private investment in the Middle East wars, was how it called
to mind American past and former politicians who seemed deeply
concerned with installing the sorts of checks and balances that today's functionaries—Summers, chief among them—have dismantled.
"The Glass-Steagall Act," said Hamza, "was made by people who
were really worried." Going back farther, even the Founders, he said,
understood just how corrupt we are; James Madison made very plain
in *Federalist* No. 10, Hamza said, that "humans have self-interest, and
that self-interest, if it's allowed to have free reign, it will be at the cost
of the public weal." And, he concluded, "they lost."

Someone brought him some milk for his tea. "This country has
been gutted," he said. Then he sized me up. "Look, you're old enough,
you know. In the African American community—there were solid
communities in the '50s and '60s—you know the families they had a
higher rate of dysfunctional families, but it was 18 percent. Now you're
looking at like 70 percent. It's crazy." I wasn't old enough to remember
the '50s and '60s, and I had to assume that what Hamza meant here by
"dysfunction" has something to do with single-motherhood, and how
presumably self-interested men have left behind so many children; if
I'm correct on this point, his statistics from the midcentury are pretty
accurate. His 70 percent is more than a third too high. Today about 52
percent of black kids live in single-mother families.

Next to Hamza was Mustafa, his handler; he held the cane Hamza
had been using, although sitting there he seemed fragile enough to
need the thing himself. He broke the mold. Mustafa was a tall, lean,
black Muslim. I'd been watching him listen to the whole conversation. Mustafa had come for this New Brunswick event from Imam
Zaid's old community in New Haven. And he was old enough to
remember the '50s and '60s; he was older, it seemed, than Hamza.
And he did know: "It's a shame," he added under his breath—all that
dysfunction.

Then came a little more of Hamza's characteristic nostalgia:
"Even the gangsters, with chains and switchblades—it wasn't Uzis."
Mustafa just nodded.

We'd been sitting near the stage at a table that had been reserved for a family who'd paid for the opportunity to be there. And just then one of the event's organizers—a local, New Jersey supporter of Zaytuna, not someone I knew from Berkeley—approached the table and asked us to take our assigned seats; they were ready to open the doors. Hamza took up his cane and seemed to be steeling himself. His eyes were off me, and conversation stopped. This would be a long day.

When I left Hamza and made my way against the crowds streaming in, I found Rasheeda pacing nervously outside the grand ballroom. She had been asked to travel with the scholars to offer her thoughts on Zaytuna's first year. Wearing a black cardigan over a typically bright, flower-patterned dress, tying it all together with a white scarf with pink stripes, Rasheeda prepared her talk. It would only be a few minutes. She also checked her phone for messages from Mahassin back at Zaytuna, who, in the days before their finals were due, had come to depend on Rasheeda to look over her work before she turned it in. We moved inside when it seemed things were getting under way.

Omar Nawaz opened the event with all the requisite appreciations, and was followed onstage by a local boy who offered a recitation from the Koran. These events always began this way. And then came a video presentation that made the case for Zaytuna once again: A "new kind of college . . . that is committed through practice, teaching, and the free exchange of ideas, to Islam's critical role in the modern world." It was promotional material I had seen before. Much of what's in the video I'd been there for. Here was the school making history. Here is a school whose time has come. Here is an idea that draws its inspiration from Islam's earliest revelations. "A little light today can illuminate the journey tomorrow." And so on.

The point is, if you were in this room, you'd almost certainly heard this message before, perhaps countless times now over the past few years. Rasheeda had long since stopped paying attention. Repeating yourself is, perhaps, an occupational hazard not only for a cleric, but also for anyone—the politician, the public radio host, the museum curator, the educator—who desperately needs private money to keep a cause or a movement growing. One thing Muslim institutions have going for them is that they are being perfectly pious when they announce at the start of every event, every solicitation, every video, that what comes next is "in the name of God, the beneficent, the merciful."

And so, as you'd expect, this is precisely what Imam Zaid did when he took the stage following the video presentation. *Bismillah ar-Rahman ar-Raheem.* He asked Allah's blessings for every mile we'd all traveled, for every hill and valley.

For him, arriving in New Brunswick was like coming home. He'd spent years at Rutgers University, and he'd studied there, sure; he'd earned a degree. But more, he recalled revitalizing the Muslim Student Association here, rabblerousing, he said, on campus and later among the Ivy Leaguers at both Columbia and Princeton, insisting that they, like Rutgers, divest from apartheid South Africa. History had been made here already, just as it was being made now at Zaytuna. Together with some of the brothers and sisters in this room, he'd gathered at a space they'd rented "right in the hood," he said, where despite "rain, snow, sleet, or hail," each day would begin and end with prayer. "I feel like I'm with family."

What Zaid—and later Rasheeda—would emphasize was that, in his words, "This is not a West Coast institution. It is a national institution." The students came from everywhere, including right here. Mahassin Muhsin, "a very promising scholar," Zaid said, was from nearby Trenton. He looked out to find her parents in the crowd. They stood and were recognized.

For too long, perhaps, Zaytuna had been known for its place and impact in free-spirited, Sufi-friendly California. This was Sheikh Hamza's legacy. And while maintaining the name as they transitioned from the institute to the college offered any number of advantages—not least of which was the name recognition that went along with Imam Zaid Shakir and Sheikh Hamza Yusuf—they seemed to worry that they'd not yet shaken the sense people had that Zaytuna was just an outgrowth of the community in Hayward, or, to some degree perhaps, that it belonged mainly to Muslims in Berkeley, San Francisco, and Oakland. Anyone else was an interloper. For Zaytuna's sake, attracting the best students and carrying out the best fund-raising would require that they change this perception about the school, however weak or strong it remained.

When she followed her teacher to the podium, Rasheeda would repeat Imam Zaid's pattern almost exactly, although she would raise the stakes to include what she'd learned at Zaytuna about Muhammad. Speaking of herself and her classmates, she said: "The thing we were attracted to was not a Bay Area thing; it was a Prophetic thing." While talking together at year's end about what each of them gained over the year, what the students discovered they'd taken from Zaytuna was the sense that family and community—like the kind Zaid remembered here in New Brunswick—was what the school was actually all about. And they were eager to see it grow beyond themselves. That is what made Zaytuna Prophetic, because "connecting the heart" to others will help you "build the community, work for the community," which, as she put it, was "how the Prophet lived." Here was another lesson she'd learned in Sheikh Hamza's Prophetic Biography.

So, apparently, was the kind of earnest salesmanship and enthusiasm it takes to build new religious institutions in this world. "On behalf of the students," she concluded, "believe me we are very thankful for the support we have from the Muslim community. And we desperately need more support. This is a community effort. We need you. So thank you for being here. And thank you."

Zaytuna had prepared a second video, to show the New Brunswick community just what, and mainly who, they would be supporting. It began, of course, with the scrolling caption "In the name of God, the beneficent, the merciful." Over the course of just a few minutes, Sheikh Hamza would appear, along with Imam Zaid and Dr. Hatem—all filmed in the classroom. There were also clips of a series of scholars the school had invited for talks throughout the year, major figures in the Muslim world including the saint Habib Umar bin Hafiz, Swiss professor Tariq Ramadan, Sherman Jackson, Duke University's Ebrahim Moosa, and Sylviane Diouf, a historian of the West African slave trade and Muslim migrations throughout the Americas. Appearing one after another, without any specific audio, these influential scholars suggested the growing social and intellectual capital behind Zaytuna. The video seems to ask: What if this were the school's permanent faculty? What if Zaytuna could afford all this?

But this possibility was just a footnote to the real focus of the presentation, the faces of the school as it was in year one. There was Chris Cusano seated in his room with a stack of books, reflecting back to the convocation, when he and the rest of Zaytuna walked out into the assembled crowd, when he realized that despite the name and its years of success under Sheikh Hamza, suddenly all the pressure was on them. "It's the grand opening of the school," he says in the video, "but at the same time it's: Who are the students and are they going to succeed?" With the first academic year nearly behind them, that still seemed an open question, which was, in a way, exactly as the founders wanted it. There was no guarantee; the caption under Chris's name—"Zaytuna College, Class of 2014"—was something to aspire to. They'd been saying it all along, going back years now, and we'd all just heard it from Rasheeda, the success of students like her or Chris depended on the community.

Then there was Haroon, who had come to Zaytuna to take his religion seriously—"to better my relationship with God," he said—wanting to immerse himself completely in an Islamic environment. Back home in Sterling Heights—which it should be noted is one of only a handful of American cities with a Muslim population of more than one hundred thousand—he says, "it's easy to take your religion for granted. But here, I take it seriously now. . . . And when you're passionate about something you want to be the best at it."

Veronica Hernandez, whom I'd spent very little time with, had taken from her experience of this year a lesson about intention, that knowledge for knowledge's sake is an empty pursuit. She'd seen at Zaytuna the combination of education and lifestyle; together, the students would work and pray, study and eat. "There's a meaning in everything that you do, *insha'Allah*."

Leenah would put it most succinctly. "Zaytuna is everything for me. Everything revolves around Zaytuna, to be honest with you. . . . And if anything, I'd want to take every moment that's passed back." Having taken a lesson from her teachers, Leenah was feeling nostalgia for something she'd only just started.

And the school was playing on this nostalgia. The video showed candid moments, many in slow motion, of the students bearing huge and growing smiles. There was Sumaya perfecting her Arabic in response to Imam Zaid's instruction. The women with their books were gathered on couches in the lounge. Rasheeda shelved books in the library. They prayed in Arabic on the grounds of the Baptist seminary, folding their hands. Adnan laughed while leading class from the instructor's place at the front of the classroom.

As for Adnan, who was also interviewed for the video and asked to reflect on this first year, the most impressive thing about Zaytuna was something we'd actually talked about very early on, which was not a lesson about himself or the pursuit of knowledge; it wasn't about community, really, or about perfecting a single line of Arabic. In fact, his lesson was only about Islam insofar as that's what he was faced with every day. "Over the course of my year here at Zaytuna, I would say I've actually grown deeper to appreciate the breadth of Islam," he said. "There is a vast ocean of scholarly opinion about any one subject, so when you come here you get to taste some of those opinions and you begin to become appreciative of the difference and diversity that our religion has."

For these students, Zaytuna can offer only some of what Islam might mean; being there is just the beginning of coming to terms with just how different we all are. And when Hartford Seminary's Ingrid Mattson, the first convert and first woman ever elected president of the Islamic Society of North America, calls Zaytuna "the most important thing happening in America," this must be why. The school is already imparting the greatest and simplest truth any of our religions present us with. Hamza has said it in the classroom: *Every thought that comes to your mind, God is other than that.* The only thing worth worshipping is the thing we don't already know.

It was the same basic setup all year: A meal was served to a crowd of hundreds of Muslims—if not more than a thousand—who had gathered inside the grand ballroom of a major American hotel chain to hear Hamza and Zaid speak about their college. This time the invitations had said, "Zaytuna College, Year One: Making Faith and Learning

Coexist." At some point during the proceedings, after the room had prayed and been fed, after they'd listened to several speeches— including Zaid's but not yet Hamza's; that would be dessert—there would be time set apart for fund-raising.

A goal would be set; today's was $400,000. The community would be told they had come to help change their own condition. Zaytuna had called on Ahmed Bedier, a civil rights advocate and founder of the Tampa-based civic engagement organization United Voices for America, "to come and speak to you and help you part with your money and still feel good about it afterwards." Bedier, who hosts a weekly global-affairs talk show on Tampa's NPR affiliate, put his mission in this context: "We're not being treated like the best of nations," he said, "because we're not living up to our role. . . . We're not acting like the best of nations. . . . We're not leading like the best of nations. . . . We're not being who Allah wants us to be. . . . This is not a problem with the Taliban. This is not a problem somewhere else. This is a world-wide Muslim problem." And Zaytuna, which this crowd could support with their donations, represented part of the answer.

When Bedier took the stage he set benchmarks, and he set them high: "I'm looking for one champion, or more, that will say, 'I believe in the promise of Allah . . . and right now I am going to pledge $50,000.'"

Bedier then had a seat. But he wasn't seated for long.

After just thirty seconds, a man at table 11 raised his hand.

And Bedier, whose made-for-radio voice, in its higher registers, sounds remarkably like Wallace Shawn's, called out: *Takbir!*

The crowd called back: *Allahu akbar!*

This call and response was a pattern I'd seen all year at events like this. And so Bedier continued: "Who will also rise," he said, "to the challenge and say, 'I want to be with the other donor, in the same place in the hereafter and get the same rewards'?" Silence. He tried again: "Zaytuna is in the business so they can save people, so they can save our children!"

And when, after several more minutes of encouragement and needling of a fairly sedate crowd, an anonymous donor turned in a pledge sheet with $50,000 written across it, they all joined in once again.

Fifty-thousand dollars! *Takbir!*

Allahu akbar!

Maashaa Allah! And God is good.

This fund-raising went on for more than thirty minutes, and Bedier complained around the midway point as the dessert came out and he lost the crowd's focus. Each time the giving slowed he would either raise the stakes or lower the size of donation he was seeking. He continued to remind the audience of the condition of the *ummah* throughout the Muslim world, those fighting and dying under the suppression of despots, those others who in just eighteen days had ended the twenty-nine-year reign of Egypt's Hosni Mubarak. Eventually, Sheikh Hamza got up from his table and wandered with his cane to a far corner of the stage, where he took a seat. He didn't say a word. His presence was enough. And with ten $10,000 donations Bedier quickly raised another quarter of their goal. "We should ask ourselves," he said, "why American Muslims have such opportunity and wealth and prosperity. . . . Allah is testing us with the wealth and the pleasures of life." The grand total Bedier collected was about $245,000, which seemed not bad for less than an hour's work. And they'd done this all once already the previous day on Long Island. Entrance into the ballroom itself had cost everyone here at least $95. If you paid at the door, it was $110. Although, as always, that had mainly been for what was coming next. Sheikh Hamza Yusuf would take the stage.

It had been wrong since the beginning, Hamza admitted. The mistake was something he probably should have noticed. For the first decade of Zaytuna's existence, the logo they'd created featuring an olive tree and a minaret included a waning crescent moon over the horizon. In Islam, the moon should be waxing. Somebody noticed, Hamza said in his introductory remarks. "Everything changed after that. It's been waxing since."

He'd used his cane to get there and his voice might have cracked once or twice, but on stage Sheikh Hamza seemed transformed. He'd get the crassness of asking for money out of the way immediately, with a few uncharacteristically clipped phrases: "I have to tell you.

We need your help. We need your support. This institute is growing. We need to hire. We need infrastructure." No one liked to ask
for money, but at Zaytuna no one seemed to like it less than Hamza.

But soon he was on his way as a preacher. The sheikh's theme was
education. And Hamza began with the Prophet, who, he said, quoting
a portion of the hadith, had "only come to teach"—not to fight, not to
conquer, but to teach. For Muslims, it was the Prophet himself who
had made the moral life an essential piece of learning—"inextricably
bound in the tradition." And for more than a century, the moral life
had been an essential part of American education, too. But once
again, as Hamza presented it, that was no longer the case. We're in
a downward spiral, he said, that had been accelerating since he was
young. The only good news about this year in America's schools is
that they're better now than they will be next year. The bad news, of
course, is that they're worse now than they were the year before.

The great promise of the college had been to slow and ultimately
reverse this downward trajectory, which, as Hamza proceeded,
seemed an increasingly urgent prospect. He used another favorite
metaphor, of the two sticks municipalities often plant alongside a
sapling tree "to bind it so that it grows straight." This was the true
purpose of education, the true hope of a liberal arts degree, to make
upright and moral citizens. In Islam, this would mean that knowledge
was for Allah. The use of knowledge to impress anyone else—to turn
heads, as Hamza said—"will take people to the hellfire."

So, when it came to offering support to the nation's first Muslim
college, these were the stakes. Sheikh Hamza's every word over the
next hour would be in defense of this cause. Failure, as he presented
it, looked calamitous. The downward spiral moved toward hell.

I'd heard darkness in his sermons before, but this afternoon was
beginning to feel harrowing and, by the sheikh's own definition, prophetic. "The Prophets," he would say, "are people on the road to
hell in this world who are saying, 'Stop. Turn around. This is not the
place you want to go.'" He told the crowd he'd just finished a paper
mapping the afterlife, which was based on traditional accounts of the
Prophet's own dreamlike night journey into the afterlife. His own
writing seemed to have darkened his outlook.

He'd told the crowd at the outset that he wanted to move through three topics—education, where we are, and where we're going—in succession. Within minutes, though, he was quoting the scholarly giant Imam al-Ghazzali's book on death, and he offered no apology for cutting right to the chase: where we're going. "I didn't want to talk about it yet, but I'm already there. Because it's just staring us right in the eyes." Al-Ghazzali had said, Hamza explained, that "none of you exist except that you will go to hell." (Even Facebook was a den of vice, "designed by some computer geniuses not to find potential spouses, but to find potential sources of sin. Literally designed to get girls to put up their pictures, put up what their hobbies are, and then you could meet them online, and A leads to B and B leads to C and before you know it you're at H, which stands for H-E-L-L.")

The prophets, he would say, did what they did out of compassion, warning us of how Allah would judge everyone for the lives they lead in this world. The prophets warned us of everlasting punishments by pointing to the degradation all around us. What has always driven the prophets, he said, is love. "They don't want to see people fall into the pit." *Stop*, the prophets say. *Turn around*. Although today it was very clearly Hamza saying this.

"And that's why there are people in hell, right now, in New Brunswick," he said. "There are people in hell. You have crack addicts right here in this town. These people are living in hell. And they're living in hell because of conditions and environments, because there were not people there to guide them. There weren't the sticks there to keep them straight when they were young, when they were budding. There were not the educators that had the moral decency to recognize that these are human beings. They need good schools. They need good families. They need education. They need jobs. They need recreation. All of these things. They were ignored and neglected."

This was our doing, he seemed to be saying. This hell was our creation. It hadn't been a choice, he would say, though we had been free to choose. But all our choices are to do good. To evil like this we can only capitulate. And there is nothing worse, he went on, than continuing to give in to an educational system that is failing our children by refusing to instill in them a sense of basic human decency.

The matter was, as usual with Hamza, intensely personal. "And I swear to God," he said, "as Allah as my witness, I would rather that my son was an illiterate, honorable street sweeper, than that he . . . loses his way in this world, and denies his Lord, or falls into the worst forms of sin, that he becomes so defiled by this world, that even his parents don't recognize him."

He then issued the only official legal ruling, or fatwa, I'd ever heard delivered by an Islamic scholar: "If you want a fatwa from me, I really consider it prohibited by Islamic law to send a child to public school in this country."

The crowd, which had been politely rapt and silent, burst into applause.

"We're losing our children."

That we only have a short time to make good in the world had formed the basis of the school's educational worldview. It meant building things that would last. "This," he said, "is our challenge as a community. Everything that we build here will be reaped in the next life."

Knowledge for Allah's sake was the choice Hamza had always presented to his students. Zaytuna was the choice he and Zaid and Hatem had been offering the community—and ultimately the nation, whether it was ready for it or not. He was approaching the end. "This is a great opportunity we have. This time we have here in the United States of America—our community is under siege. But if you ask me it's a good thing. Because I know where it comes from."

> You're saying it comes from the Zionist lobby. Or it comes from the FBI. Or it comes from the neoconservatives. Or it comes from the right-wing Christians. . . . It's all from Allah. It's from God. He's the one that is forcing us to come to terms with the fact that we are not here to eat, to drink, to procreate, to have nice houses, to have nice cars—that's all fine and dandy. Those are accouterments. That's not the reason you're here. The reason you're here is to establish the worship of Allah in yourselves and then to invite others to it. . . . We're not here, I'm not here, to convert the United States of America to Islam. I'm not. Because I can't do anything. . . . I love this people. This is my people. This

is my home. I have to love them. This is my people. This is where I'm from.

Hamza had talked many times about the burden of his leadership and sacred knowledge in general, what al-Ghazzali would describe using yet another tree metaphor. Sacred knowledge should humble you, bend you low like a fruit tree to the ground. And if Hamza's sacred knowledge hadn't humbled him before, it now appeared that this first year of Zaytuna College, a school founded in a nation increasingly suspicious of Muslims who want to build anything, had brought him low, to dark and bewildering places, which for the Muslim scholar is just where he'd always wanted to be. It was home. It was where he was from.

9/10/11, "United We Stand"

The lobby was bright and airy, with huge glass walls letting the DC sun shine in. Washington on September 10, 2011, looked a lot like New York City on September 11, 2001. I couldn't help but look up to the high ceilings and overhead walkways. At eye level, CNN played on flat screens throughout the convention center, announcing what we've all grown quite used to CNN announcing over the years: SECURITY HEIGHTENED AMID TERROR THREAT. At the ten-year anniversary of 9/11, CNN was interspersing news of the nation's heightened alert—reporting from airports, our highways, and our public buildings—with personal stories from the day of the attacks. As a nation we were remembering as much as we were looking ahead at what still might come. On-screen, a father in a black police uniform appeared against a white background. His words appeared over his head, white on black, in closed-captioning: MY SON JIMMY WAS A FIREFIGHTER ON 9/11.

I reached Hall C of the Walter E. Washington Convention Center, site of "United We Stand," a daylong conference of lectures and panels bringing together Muslim leaders from around the country (and in some cases, the world). The early-morning crowd—the real diehards—was sparse, making the whole place seem even more cavernous. Seats were everywhere, thousands of them all facing the stage and filling up the front half of the hall. Brothers on the right, sisters on the left, families in the middle. There were placards showing you the way, which was unusual for a Zaytuna event. Conservative as Hamza Yusuf or Zaid Shakir may claim to be, this day would include Muslims even more conservative than they, whose commitment to Islam divides a massive room like this into the brothers and the sisters. I read the signs as a concession of sorts, an olive branch from Imam Zaid Shakir and Zaytuna to Yasir Qadhi's Orthodox school of thought, under the growing influence of AlMaghrib Institute. Whether Hamza Yusuf would have shared in that gesture is still an open question. "United

for Change," marking the tenth anniversary of the September 11 attacks, was Imam Zaid's event. He was the chairman.

Zaid was even thinner than the last time I'd seen him, drowning
more than usual in a dark suit and yellow shirt. Though fasting is regular practice for the imam, Ramadan, that "marathon of a month," as
Atlaf Husain, one of the conference presenters, would describe it, had
once again taken its toll on Zaid. That hike into Strawberry Canyon
had come in the days before Ramadan, when he seemed more robust;
his sermons a year earlier were all in preparation for the fast. Now,
I was encountering him at the end of that holy month. Having traveled to the other side of the country at a sacred time when he hates to
travel, Superman was diminished. Standing in front of a shimmering
backdrop on a stage decorated with bouquets, his image projected on
screens flanking the stage, Zaid resembled a world-weary Christian
televangelist from the 1980s. The room was slowly filling. I spotted
Omar Nawaz in the front row, as always seeming to lean back and sit
on the edge of his seat at the same time.

Rounding out the first session of the day, Imam Zaid offered his
reflections on the subject of mercy, which he, like so many of the
scholars and students, papers and slogans I'd encountered throughout the year, identified as the distinguishing trait of Islam. Once
again, he was receiving a hero's welcome. And after a decade of living
through what strikes this community as a kind of mercilessness—
in our communities, our politics, our economics, you name it—the
time, he said, was right for some heroism.

Zaid knows as well as anyone how his audiences see him; for most
of these followers, his superhero image will never be diminished by
sunken cheeks or the loose fit of his jacket and slacks. If the Prophet
is Zaid's example, he is theirs. Indeed, over the year, what had become most obvious about Zaid is his model relentlessness. That's
what this Superman is—a perpetual motion machine. But Zaid seems
incapable of asking of others what he asks of himself. There is no
compulsion in Islam.

And yet, despite all that we'd seen in the decade of what's been
called "Islamophobia production," with the same consistency and
force Zaid had shown throughout the year when talking to a gather-

ing of his followers, to this crowd in DC he insisted that the work to be done on behalf of American Islam must begin with American Muslims. And just as he's spoken of the founding of Zaytuna in grand historic terms—"You are making history," he'd declared over and over—he continued to speak of making a true home for Islam in America in grand heroic terms.

Heroism of the kind his speech was calling for has as its foundation real sacrifice and the compassion it takes to give preference to the needs of others. For religious types, there's nothing unusual in that, and because the bedrock of this compassion is mercy, Zaid said, the most heroic acts we can commit are merciful ones. Knowing this and acting with mercy, Zaid believes, involves a willingness to suffer deprivation—perhaps even the sort of deprivation that results from a decade of increasing Islamophobia. It's truly no wonder that the man most renowned in the West for claiming blessedness for the persecuted is known as a prophet among Muslims around the world. Zaytunies, remember, have a special place for the man known as Jesus.

But Zaid would not be happy simply with grand claims for the blessedness and heroism of those who suffer for mercy's sake. For the mercy we'd been talking about all year to have any effect on these Muslims—most especially for Zaid's students and the world around them and the country they call home—heroism must be the basis for a new understanding of politics and economics. Islamic America, in the religious imagination of Imam Zaid Shakir, has as its bedrock sacrifice and the preference of the other over the self. What this requires, Zaid went on to say, is what Napoleon Bonaparte claimed as the real struggle, or perhaps the real skill, of the hero. Napoleon put it this way: "True heroism consists in being superior to the ills of life, in whatever shape they may challenge us to combat." Combat, of course, is a dangerous word in the mouth of a Muslim leader, which may explain why Zaid decided to paraphrase: "True heroism calls us to rise above the ills around us, and inside us."

More than a dozen speakers—including Tariq Ramadan, Sherman Jackson, Imam Siraj Wahhaj, and Yasir Qadhi—had gathered to acknowledge the national significance of 9/11 before an audience that would grow all day; no matter the differences in their beliefs—

minor or major—they must all be welcomed to "be a truthful witness and tell the full story," not just of this one day, he seemed to be saying, but of the whole of American Islam. He'd said something similar to me a year earlier after my first visit to his Oakland mosque: "You're doing your part—we have to do more." By *you* he meant me, and over the year he'd called out a number of others who seemed to look at Zaytuna with kindness; he called them "fair witnesses." They were also heroes. But as always, Zaid wanted to look into the *ummah*. By *we*, he meant the Muslims—friends and enemies alike.

Along the back wall and running up the right side of the hall, vendors prepared their wares, selling incense and robes, books and more books and calligraphy, and their causes. Learn to invest the shariah way—no liquor, no gambling, no pornography, no banks. This is what I'd come to expect.

The back of the room was spread with a massive white prayer mat taped to the floor, which would be used for group prayers at designated times throughout the day, but would otherwise be a gathering place for groups of men or women to talk and laugh or a spot for kids to play with their toys. Everyone left his shoes at the edge. At least one man would find time for a nap. Another sat cross-legged with a laptop computer. But the bowing in prayer, the prostrations I'd come to know—often by practice—over my year with this community, would be ongoing during the breaks between lectures. There would never be many—two or three somewhere along the edge, close to their shoes, at any given time—but they were there meditating.

After the morning's first session I met Omar near the booth where Zaytuna had set up shop with banners, catalogs, Sheikh Hamza's books and DVDs. It was still early; the crowds were still coming. But for once Omar wasn't the man in charge, not pulled in so many directions. This wasn't his show. And yet he was most certainly on the ball, ever distracted, both where he was and already on his way to somewhere else. While we talked he was directing another Zaytuna assistant, Ali Hasan, to begin getting the fund-raising envelopes on every chair—thousands of them. All year there were always so many envelopes.

He was there to listen and learn as much as anyone, which is something we often forget about functionaries like Omar. But there they are, making things run, part of the faithful.

He was impressed by the lineup of participants, and also a little covetous: over the year, Tariq Ramadan and Sherman Jackson had both visited Zaytuna, and Omar dreamed of one day having them on the faculty. The way he talked about it, you got the sense that some of the early conversations had already taken place.

The new school year had already started and the second Zaytuna class had taken their place next to the inaugural one. They'd followed through with what Omar had explained they hoped to do, admitting younger students and a slightly smaller group. All told, they'd lost five of the original class, after all. And here he was to explain: Some of those original students just had to choose different priorities. What's more, he continued, Zaytuna was no different really than any other college, an argument he'd both been making and not making about the school since I'd met him. Every college could expect a 30 percent attrition rate. But you could tell he was disappointed. What set Zaytuna's first class apart had been the sense that everyone involved seemed convinced they were making history. Losing a third of the class—five of fifteen students—calls such a claim into question.

"United for Change" seemed, in part, like a meditation on a single verse of the Koran, from the forty-ninth surah, The Rooms: "O mankind, indeed We have created you from male and female and made you peoples and tribes that you may know one another." Whatever this *ayat*, or verse, might say about the relationship between men and women—some have used it to argue for gender equality among Muslims—or the place of Muslims in a country where they are not well known or understood, the presenters at the conference, almost to a one, used "peoples and tribes" to refer to themselves. The decade since 9/11—a decade of war in the Muslim world and of Islamophobia at home—has turned this community inward, often quite critically.

For most of my year with Zaytuna I had no faces to attach to complaints that Sheikh Hamza Yusuf made about American Muslims who could find no real allegiances here. His condemnations had always been more or less abstract, which made me assume he meant the Fort Hood shooters and underwear bombers of the world, which, in effect, he had. He did mean the violent ones. But these were the "nutcases." Even more dangerous, I'd taken him to say, because they have a platform, dedicated followers, and real reach—all of which Hamza Yusuf knows well from experience—are the Salafi teachers. Perhaps Yasir Qadhi especially.

Qadhi spoke after *asr*, the late-afternoon prayer, using his time onstage to condemn the attacks of 9/11 as both "un-Islamic and counterproductive" and to ask again that the audience—and Americans more broadly—consider where the rage that leads to extremist violence comes from. A stout and sturdy man with a full black beard, equal parts professor and preacher, Qadhi delivered a stirring speech. He emphasized the ghastly carnage and terror of 9/11—the riveting and haunting images, he said—while also describing the attacks as a "necessary catalyst" for the Muslim community. That day had shown him—and others like him—just how naive Muslims had been about their place in this country. The violence was a call to action. He was actually sounding a little like Sheikh Hamza and Imam Zaid. "Post 9/11 Muslims realized that they needed to be actively engaged in the media, in politics, and in civic service. Basically, Muslims realized that they need to be a part of the framework of the land that they live in." Once again, Qadhi "unequivocally and unconditionally" condemned those who carried out the attacks and called on every Muslim leader in the country to join him. It went without saying that everyone in that room already had, years ago.

Yasir Qadhi said that 9/11 had forced this community to grow up. He was, I recalled, the only other contemporary American Muslim leader that Hamza and I talked about that day on our way to the airport back in March. He was also perhaps the only other American Muslim figure besides Hamza and Zaid themselves with the following and the stature to pull off what Zaytuna has done over the last fifteen years and now looks to do in the decades to come. And on our drive just six months earlier from Hamza's home to the San Francisco airport, when we'd talked about Andrea Elliott's *New York Times*

Magazine profile of Qadhi and what Hamza believed was her poor handling of Qadhi's commitment to the fringe Islamic doctrine of *al-walaa wal-baraa*, he hadn't seemed nearly so open to the possibility of a day like this, with their sharing not just a stage, but also a message of unity. After all, it was that article about Qadhi that had sent Hamza down the path explaining just how dangerous he believes religion can be—in the wrong hands.

Those questions of national loyalty that Sheikh Hamza had raised with me back in March—and today, whatever unspoken implications remained—have been at the center of Muslim life in America since 9/11. For many Muslims in this country, these questions go back decades. Where do your allegiances lie? Can you believe, as a Muslim, in the political authority that shapes American laws and guides American foreign policy? And would the position be different if the American political class were doing more to defend and protect Muslims throughout the world than they currently are?

Hamza had given me his answer. Believers who cannot find it in their hearts to love the ideals of the country or whose Islamic legal reasoning prevents them from developing allegiances to America, these Muslims ought to have no place in American public life. That's not to say, he would insist, that these beliefs ought to be disrespected, or that they are not valid Islamic opinions. Sheikh Hamza had said it before: The scholarly tradition, and the history of the *ummah* itself, has always allowed that on the difficult details of the shariah, Muslims will not ever all agree.

But for the sake of the country and the Muslims who choose to live here, Sheikh Hamza was clear: If you don't believe in America, if you can't find your place here, you should go. Leave. You're not wanted here.

That was also, strangely, the chorus among protesters at Park51; it's what Ebad Rahman and his friends had heard in the hours after 9/11 as they marched away from disaster. Indeed, confronting that chorus is what had sent Ebad looking for answers at Zaytuna in the first place. What can it mean for Zaytuna when that's the sentiment coming from its most celebrated founder—arguably the most influential Muslim scholar in the West?

"United for Change" was officially a moment for the *ummah* in the West to set their differences aside; it was the time and place, everyone seemed to agree, for leaders like Yasir Qadhi and Tariq Ramadan, and of course Zaytuna's founders Hamza and Zaid, to settle on their common ground. Everyone there had been for ten years condemning the violence of 9/11. And that message was clear once again. But the Islam that united these people this day was no longer a tradition that could be hijacked. That metaphor no longer worked. The Islam on display, the Islam that brought all these people together, would not allow it.

An early speaker, Howard University's Altaf Husain, had set the stage with a focus on what he repeatedly referred to as "the cult of terror," made up of men who were spiritually void. To suggest that these men, or any extremists, could hijack the religion was an insult; it would be to accept the dangerous premise that Islam itself is susceptible to such treatment. "Islam," Husain insisted, "is not at fault." Muhammad taught self-control, self-restraint, and mercy, he said.

This mercy is what I've been hearing about all year; it's what Zaid had begun the day with. And the heightened spirituality that mercy itself requires—that true Islam requires, he would say—is what those hijackers could not possibly achieve.

Altaf Husain also made clear from the very earliest moments of the day another goal "United for Change" set out to accomplish. This is also the part of the American Muslim response to 9/11 that many of these leaders and scholars had found most difficult in the years immediately following the attacks. It had been natural for Hamza Yusuf to condemn the violence of 9/11 when called on to advise President Bush in the lead-up to war in October 2001—or for any of these leaders, many of whom first found a public platform, or a public calling, only after 9/11, in written statements issued after the attacks, or from their place in the mosque or when interviewed on TV. Those early days saw the birth of the metaphor that said "Islam has been hijacked."

This day saw its death. Ten years later, they all seemed to agree with Yasir Qadhi that it was no longer enough to hold accountable the "cult of terror" that brought about the violence of 9/11. The "cult of terror" had coalesced around a rage in the Muslim world that America had ignored in the years before the attacks, and since the attacks it had been a form of unpatriotic sacrilege even to address that rage—especially as an American Muslim. What was perhaps worse, or what had unquestionably deepened the anger and widened the rift keeping the Muslim community in the United States from their neighbors, was the fact that the "cult of terror" had led to a "war on terror," a tragic overreaction that resulted in the longest war in US history and the upending of thousands—even hundreds of thousands—of lives, lives of their brothers and sisters and children.

After the evening prayer but before the last session of the day, I stepped out for air and saw the only police action the conference had attracted that day. At the south entrance to the convention center, a U-Haul van had been stopped; the police were midsearch, it seemed, as I approached. Two young men, one with a beard, seemed to be moving some equipment. A cruiser and a police SUV had their lights spinning, bouncing off the church across the street and in through the windows of the convention center. The driver and his passenger stood on the sidewalk and appeared simply to be waiting to be let go.

As I made my way in for the final session, the security guard who greeted me at the top of the stairs seemed to read my mind. We looked at each other. We looked outside. The police were for once leaving the Muslims alone.

While much of the day had seemed reserved for building up the community from within—and with a message about Muslim American unity post-9/11—Hamza's address as the day came to a close once again offered a version of what he'd been saying all year in support of the college.

Ultimately, Hamza's force as a scholar and religious leader remains what it has always been—his personality and passion for knowledge—which is part of the reason his videos and recordings from a decade ago remain powerful today. You can still see the same man. There's no denying his grasp and commitment to the tradition. You see it in his flow from English to Arabic—often translating himself—without ever missing a beat. And to comment on the force of Hamza's personality is not exactly the same as pointing to a "cult of personality"—despite the group of followers who gather around him for a word, an autograph, a blessing, the moment he arrives and finds his place in the front row of seats. Breaking through that scrum had proved difficult all year, whether the crowd gathered were Zaytuna students or his followers around the country. Even this night while waiting my turn to greet him before he was called finally to the stage—he had the honored last slot of the evening—I was again asked politely by one event organizer if I wouldn't mind finding my seat. Hamza's traveling handler Mustafa, whom I'd met in New Jersey, looked on as well from the foot of the steps leading to the stage. Someone is always looking out for Hamza Yusuf because someone is always trying to touch him, to take with them a little bit of his sainthood. And the saint is always at risk. Photographers shoot him from every possible angle.

The talk he promised this evening, "United We Stand: One Destiny," began again with the question: Where are we going? But his answer was immediately clear. In some ways, it was the same answer he'd been giving all year: If we're going anywhere, we're going with *him*. And he's aware that there is some anxiety about that among those gathered. By Hamza's own account, he's tried to be true to his own understanding of the tradition; but, as he's said before, he may be too conservative for some in the audience and too liberal for others.

It may have been only the other speakers' consistency of approach—if not entirely in their content—that made Hamza's presentation contrast so starkly. Where Altaf Husain began the day with passing references to his family's travels with him, which explained nothing more than his somewhat late arrival (Zaid: "Yes, family might slow you down!" Husain: "No, I might slow *them* down!"), Hamza found in stories about his children actual relevant lessons for the entire community regarding government overreach, the TSA, and a warning about the increasing threat to all our children in the form of pedophilia. As Hamza tells the story of his most recent trip to Saudi Arabia, with his young son facing a pat-down from a male TSA agent, he almost came to blows. In his ongoing study of pornography, he had learned that child molesters were overwhelmingly male. "You're not laying your hands on that six-year-old boy," he said. "If you do, you'd better get your Taser ready"—an unwise re-mark, perhaps, coming from a Muslim man holding a boarding pass for Saudi Arabia. But his son was cleared to fly after a pat-down by a female agent.

And even with this—and it's true the sheikh had much, much more to say—Hamza was speaking to a community that would see in a confrontation at the airport the deepening of Muslim roots in the nation. There is always something saintly to admire in stories of the personal and family life of Hamza Yusuf—even when the story ends with something as profane as his standing his ground out of fear of pedophilia. By the end and his final blessing of peace, the audience was again in tears.

And from my place once more in the audience, even as I joined in with genuine applause for the sheikh, I was still left with this to consider. Hamza Yusuf is the founder of a Western liberal arts college who remains skeptical that Western education is capable of producing the kinds of scholars—indeed, the kinds of Muslims—America needs. He's the most well-known and most influential Muslim American scholar in a community in need of unity and direction, an entire community that today had taken this remembrance of 9/11 as a reason to look inward and reform itself. And yet, once again, Hamza's message begins and ends with him.

This all makes me think that in the end one of two things is happening. Sheikh Hamza Yusuf is either attempting to carry his community and his school forward on the strength of his own story, or he's creating his own singular brand of Islam that's at risk of being overtaken by a community—by Zaytuna, an institution of his own making—that's gathering on all sides and may someday leave him behind.

For now, though, it's clear; Hamza Yusuf is still out front and center, leading the way home.

AUTHOR'S NOTE

American colleges are, both as a matter of course and as required in most cases by federal law, protective of their students' privacy. If a father reaches out to me, for instance, with a request to know how his daughter is performing in one of my classes, or whether she's doing all she can to land that internship at *Teen Vogue*, the Family Educational Rights and Privacy Act prohibits me from discussing those details with him without her consent (unless she's under eighteen, which is almost never the case). At the institutional level, for instance, when it was reported in early 2012 that the New York City Police Department had been surveilling Muslim Student Associations at more than a dozen schools throughout the Northeast, university presidents such as Columbia's Lee Bollinger, Yale's Richard Levin, and New York University's John Sexton all leveled sharp criticism. The consequences of the surveillance, especially those that reduce the "free and peaceful exchange of ideas . . . even of genuinely controversial ideas," Sexton emphasized, "are disquieting to our students and their families, harmful to our community-building efforts, and antithetical to the values we as a university cherish most highly." One such value, of course, is the students' right to privacy. It's a value I also believe in.

This is all to say that when I arrived at Zaytuna and began interacting with members of the inaugural class, I had to bear in mind two things: it's every school's job to protect their students from intrusive reporter-types like me, and it's any student's prerogative to ask me to leave him alone. And in the spirit of full disclosure, I'm saying this: At Zaytuna's request, I collected consent forms from students I hoped to spend any appreciable time with during the 2010–11 academic year. None of them were under eighteen. And of the fifteen students who participated in the August convocation, ten agreed to take an active part in what you've been reading. Of those who did not, only two kept their distance entirely; they would also leave the college after the first semester. The other three were all certainly cordial, and no one, to my knowledge, ever took issue with my being on campus; they seemed simply to enjoy their privacy.

One other point of disclosure: Over the course of my reporting, so that I could have access to recorded and live-streaming videos on the college's website, which they archive for donors they call their "Companions," I donated one dollar per month to Zaytuna.

Finally, for the sake of consistency, I have silently standardized Arabic spellings within a few quotations.

ACKNOWLEDGMENTS

This book would not have been possible without the help and generosity of many people. My thanks go first to Ebadur Rahman, who not only put Zaytuna College on my radar, but also eased my introduction to the growing community of Zaytunies. Ebad and I also spent many hours in conversation about the school, and he provided both a wide assortment of research materials and any number of thoughtful insights—and even specific facts—when I asked.

At Zaytuna College, I was welcomed by Omar Nawaz, who regularly inquired about my reporting, sat for hours of interviews, and made every possible effort to aid in my research. Imam Dawood Yasin invited me into my first Zaytuna College classroom and was an invaluable resource throughout my research and writing. I am grateful to Abdullah bin Hamid Ali and other Zaytuna scholars for their time and their invitations to watch them teach. Ali Malik was a kind and knowledgeable guide around the college, the mosque, and the highways of Northern California. Najeeb Hasan offered smart and sound advice in our regular conversations. My discussions with Zachary Twist were some of the very best I had throughout my time in the Bay Area. Special thanks, as well, to my friends Maryam Kashani and Sumaya Jeeva. None of my reporting would have been possible without assistance from the support staff at Zaytuna, including Sadaf

Khan, Georgia Gonzales, Haroon Sellers, Ali Hassan, Saher Qadri, Marina Omar, and a host of others at the school. My thanks go, as well, to the students whose stories I have shared in these pages.

Usama Canon and all those I met at Ta'leef Collective offered a warm welcome to their transformative community. I was received with equal openness at the Lighthouse Mosque in Oakland and the Muslim Community Center of East Bay in Pleasanton. I am also grateful for my time with scholars and leaders at the Graduate Theological Union, including Sister Marianne Farina of the Dominican School of Philosophy and Theology, Munir Jiwa of the Center for Islamic Studies, and Paul Martin of the America Baptist Seminary of the West.

I am, of course, especially grateful to the founders of Zaytuna College for opening their doors: Sheik Hamza Yusuf, Imam Zaid Shakir, and Dr. Hatem Bazian.

I would like to thank my editor, Amy Caldwell, for her careful attention and thoughtful advice as I researched and wrote this book. Her editorial assistant, Will Myers, deserves many thanks, as well. Others at Beacon, including director Helene Atwan, Pamela MacColl, Tom Hallock, Susan Lumenello, Marcy Barnes, and Gabi Anderson, have all made working with the press a great pleasure. Melissa Dobson proved an expert copy editor.

Jim Rutman is a steadfast supporter and supremely thoughtful and kind agent. He is lucky to have the support of a wonderful assistant, Dwight Curtis.

I received generous institutional support from the New School and the Gallatin School of Individualized Study at New York University.

Other friends and colleagues, editors and journalists, to whom I owe special thanks include Amy Bebergal, Peter Bebergal, Sara Burningham, Caitlin Esch, Alissa Figueroa, Evan Goldstein, Emily Guzzardi, Barbara Bradley Hagerty, George Hamilton, Dylan Kidd, Imam Khalid Latif, Elizabeth Little, Michael Krasny, Alia Malik, Haroon Moghul, Richard Parks, Eboo Patel, Llewellyn Powers, M. Ryan Purdy, Hussein Rashid, Nathan Schneider, Jeff Sharlet, and